Take Heart

Take Heart

A Daybook of Devotion

Elisabeth Day Douglas
and Judy Dunn

Copyright © 2012 Black Dog & Leventhal Publishers, Inc.

Published by Tess Press,
An imprint of Black Dog & Leventhal Publishers, Inc.
151 West 19th Street
New York, NY 10011

Manufactured in China

Cover design by Red Herring Design

ISBN: 978-1-60376-082-9

h g f e d c b a

A Daybook of Devotion

Lives of great men all remind us
We can make our lives sublime,
And, departing, leave behind us
Footprints on the sands of time;
Footprints, that perhaps another,
Sailing o'er life's solemn main,
A forlorn and shipwrecked brother,
Seeing, shall take heart again.
Let us, then, be up and doing,
With a heart for any fate;
Still achieving, still pursuing,
Learn to labour and to wait.

HENRY WADSWORTH LONGFELLOW

Take Heart is an enduringly lovely and eloquent source of reassurance, inspiration, and comfort. This daybook of devotion is designed to provide readers of all denominations with passages on a wide range of topics to help readers navigate life's most treasured and troubling moments. Special selections of scripture drawn from the New International Version of the Bible, literature, and personal writings focus on milestones and subjects such as family, loss, birth, renewal, love and marriage.

January

January 1

The least of you will become a thousand,
the smallest a mighty nation:
I am the Lord; in its time I will do this swiftly.
ISAIAH 60:22

That daily quarter of an hour, for now forty years or more, I am sure has been one of the greatest sustenances and sources of calm for my life. Of course, such "reading" is hardly reading in the ordinary sense of the word at all. As well could you call the letting a very slowly dissolving lozenge melt imperceptibly in your mouth "eating." Such reading is, of course, meant as directly as possible to feed the heart, to fortify the will—to put these into contact with God—thus, by the book, to get away from the book to the realities it suggests—the longer the better. And above all, perhaps it excludes, by its very object, all criticism, all going off on one's own thoughts as, in any way, antagonistic to the book's thoughts; and this, not by any unreal (and most dangerous) forcing of oneself to swallow, or to "like." What does not attract one's simply humble self, but (on the contrary) by a gentle passing by, by an instinctive ignoring of what does not suit one's soul. This passing by should be without a trace of would—be objective judging; during such reading we are out simply and solely to feed our own poor soul, such as it is hic et nunc. What repels or confuses us now may be the very food of angels; it may even still become the light to our own poor souls in this world's dimness. We must exclude none of such possibilities, the "infant crying for the fight" has nothing to do with more than just humbly finding, and then using, the little light that it requires.

I need not say that I would not restrict you to only one quarter of an hour a day. You might find two such helpful. But I would not exceed the fifteen minutes at any one time; you would sink to ordinary reading, if you did.

—BARON FRIEDRICH VON HUGEL

January 2

One thing I ask of the Lord,
this is what I seek:
that I may dwell in the house of the Lord
all the days of my life,
to gaze upon the beauty of the Lord
and to seek him in his temple.
For in the day of trouble,
he will keep me safe in his dwelling;
he will hide me in the shelter of his tabernacle
and set me high upon a rock.
PSALMS 27:4-5

The problem, often not discovered until late in life, is that when you look for things in life like love, meaning, motivation, it implies they are sitting behind a tree or under a rock. The most successful people in life recognize, that in life they create their own love, they manufacture their own meaning, they generate their own motivation. For me, I am driven by two main philosophies, know more today about the world than I knew yesterday. And lessen the suffering of others. You'd be surprised how far that gets you.

—NEIL DEGRASSE TYSON

January 3

. . . and your strength will equal your days.
DEUTERONOMY 33:25

If as a flower doth spread and die,
Thou would'st extend me to some good,
Before I were by frost's extremity
Nipt in the bud;
The sweetness and the praise were Thine;
But the extension and the room,
Which in Thy garland I should fill, were mine,
At Thy great doom.

For as Thou dost impart Thy grace,
The greater shall our glory be.
The measure of our joys is in this place,
The stuff with Thee.

Let me not languish then, and spend
A life as barren to Thy praise
As is the dust, to that which life doth tend,
But with delays.

All things are busy; only I
Neither bring honey with the bees,
Nor flowers to make that, nor the husbandry
To water these.

I am no link of Thy great chain,
But all my company is a weed,
Lord! place me in Thy concert; give one strain
To my poor reed.
GEORGE HERBERT

When you find your path, you must not be afraid. You need to have sufficient courage to make mistakes. Disappointment, defeat, and despair are the tools God uses to show us the way.

—PAULO COELHO

January 4

If we sin, we are Thine, knowing Thy power: but we will not sin, knowing that we are counted Thine. For to know Thee is perfect righteousness yea, to know Thy power is the root of immortality.
WISDOM OF SOLOMON 15:2-3

Anybody can rise to a crisis and face a crushing tragedy with courage, but to meet the petty hazards of the day with a laugh— I really think that requires spirit!

—JEAN WEBSTER

Imagine that the universe is a great spinning engine. You want to stay near the core of the thing—right in the hub of the wheel—not out at the edges where all the wild whirling takes place, where you can get frayed and crazy. The hub of calmness—that's your heart. That's where God lives within you. So stop looking for answers in the world. Just keep coming back to that center and you'll always find peace.

—ELIZABETH GILBERT

January 5

. . . you also, like living stones,
are being built into a spiritual house.
I PETER 2:5

Thirty years ago my older brother, who was ten years old at the time, was trying to get a report written on birds that he'd had three months to write, which was due the next day. We were out at our family cabin in Bolinas, and he was at the kitchen table close to tears, surrounded by binder paper and pencils and unopened books about birds, immobilized by the hugeness of the task ahead. Then my father sat down beside him put his arm around my brother's shoulder, and said, "Bird by bird, buddy. Just take it bird by bird."
—ANNE LAMOTT

You never know what's around the corner. It could be everything.
Or it could be nothing. You keep putting one foot in front of the
other, and then one day you look back and you've climbed a
mountain.

—TOM HIDDLESTON

January 6

*We have to be braver than we think we can be, because God is
constantly calling us to be more than we are.*
MADELEINE L'ENGLE

*Our talents are the gift that God gives to us...
What we make of our talents is our gift back to God.*
LEO BUSCAGLIA

Protect and keep the soul of me the meanest of Thy servants
amidst so many dangers of this corruptible life, and by Thy grace
accompanying me direct it along the way of peace to its home of
everlasting brightness.

—THOMAS A. KEMPIS

January 7

*... and his incomparably great power for us who believe.
That power is like the working of his mighty strength.*
EPHESIANS 1:19

A root set in the finest soil, in the best climate, and blessed with
all that sun and air and rain can do for it, is not in so sure a way
of its growth to perfection, as every man may whose spirit aspires
after all that which God ready and infinitely desirous to give him.
For the sun meets not the springing bud that stretches towards
him with half that certainty, as God, the source of all good,
communicates Himself to the soul that longs to partake of Him.

—WILLIAM LAW

January 8

Therefore, as we have opportunity,
let us do good unto all people. . . .
GALATIANS 6:10

Keep on loving each other as brothers.
HEBREWS 13:1

In terms of days and moments lived, you'll never again be as young as you are right now, so spend this day, the youth of your future, in a way that deflects regret. Invest in yourself. Have some fun. Do something important. Love somebody extra. In one sense, you're just a kid, but a kid with enough years on her to know that every day is priceless.

—VICTORIA MORAN

January 9

Then they asked him,
"What must we do to do the works the works God requires?"
JOHN 6:28

To live with purpose,
To say the courageous thing,
To celebrate the simple gift,
To follow your dreams,
This is a happy life.
WAYLAND HENRY

Begin the day by offering it and yourself to God. Look at the day as an individual thing that begins and ends with completeness in itself; then take this thing, this day and offer it to God to be a day for His use. . . . The day at once becomes a unity and life becomes unified. However many distracting details come into the day, both mind and emotion are dominated, not by them, but by the sense that you have only one thing to do—namely, to act in obedience to God with regard to them.

—GEORGE S. STEWART

January 10

*From the rising of the sun to the place where it sets,
the name of the Lord is to be praised.*
PSALMS 113:3

Your heart's voice is your true voice. It is easy to ignore it, for sometimes it says what we'd rather it did not—and it is so hard to risk the things we have. But what life are we living, if we don't live by our hearts? Not a true one. And the person living it is not the true you.

—SUSAN FLETCHER

January 11

I will be glad and rejoice in your love;
for you saw my affliction and knew
the anguish of my soul.
PSALMS 31:7

Life is an opportunity, benefit from it.
Life is beauty, admire it.
Life is a dream, realize it.
Life is a challenge, meet it.
Life is a duty, complete it.
Life is a game, play it.
Life is a promise, fulfill it.
Life is sorrow, overcome it.
Life is a song, sing it.
Life is a struggle, accept it.
Life is a tragedy, confront it.
Life is an adventure, dare it.
Life is luck, make it.
Life is too precious, do not destroy it.
Life is life, fight for it.
MOTHER TERESA

The remarkable thing about the way in which people talk about God, or about their relation to God, is that it seems to escape them completely that God hears what they are saying. A man says: "At the moment I have not the time or the necessary recollection to think about God, but later on perhaps." Or better still—a young man says, "I am too young now; first of all I will enjoy life-and then." Would it be possible to talk like that if one realized that God heard one?

—SØREN KIERKEGAARD

January 12

May the words of my mouth and the meditation of my heart, be pleasing in your sight, O Lord, my Rock and my Redeemer.
PSALMS 19:14

. . . observe for thyself what place best agrees with thy spirit; whether within doors, or without. Isaac's example in "going out to meditate in the field" will, I believe, best suit with most. Our Lord so much used a solitary garden that even Judas, when he came to betray Him, knew where to find Him: and though He took His disciples thither with Him, yet He was "withdrawn from them" for more secret devotions. . . . So that Christ had His accustomed place, and consequently accustomed duty, and so must we; He hath a place that is solitary, whither He retireth Himself, even from His own disciples, and so must we; His meditations go farther than His words, they affect and pierce His heart and soul, and so must ours. Only there is a wide difference in the object: Christ meditates on the sufferings that our sins had deserved, so that the wrath of His Father passed through all His soul; but we are to meditate on the glory He hath purchased, that the love of the Father, and the joy of the Spirit, may enter at our thoughts, revive our affections, and overflow our souls.

—RICHARD BAXTER

January 13

Brothers,
do not slander one another.
JAMES 4:2

Get rid of all bitterness, rage and anger,
brawling and slander,
along with every form of malice.
EPHESIANS 4:31

Because others are weak, should we be less careful to give them their due? You who complain so much of what others make you suffer, do you think that you cause others no pain? You who are so annoyed at your neighbour's defects, are you perfect? How astonished you would be if those whom you call evil at should make all the comments that they might upon you. But even if the whole world were to bear testimony in your favor, God, who knows all, who has seen all your faults, could confound you with a word; and does it never come into your mind to fear lest He should demand of you why you had not exercised towards your brother a little of that mercy which He, who is your Master, so abundantly bestows on you?

—FENELON

January 14

I urge, then, first of all, that requests, prayers, intercession and
thanksgiving be made for everyone—for kings and all
those in authority, that we may live peaceful and quiet lives in
all godliness and holiness.
1 TIMOTHY 2:1-2

There comes a moment in life when you say to yourself—enough. This is ENOUGH! Then—you take a walk with your destiny. To change. To fulfill your purpose. We all have it. But are you willing to take that first step?

—BESA KOSOVA

January 15

Your word is a lamp to my feet and a light for my path.
PSALMS 119:105

Between us and Thyself remove
Whatever hindrances may be,
That so our inmost heart may prove
A holy temple, meet for Thee.
LATIN MASS OF 15TH CENTURY

There are only two ways to live your life. One is as though nothing is a miracle. The other is as though everything is a miracle.

—ALBERT EINSTEIN

Miracles are a retelling in small letters of the very same story which is written across the whole world in letters too large for some of us to see.

—C.S. LEWIS

January 16

I have fought the good fight, I have finished the race, I have kept the faith. Now there is in store for me the crown of righteousness, which the Lord, the righteous Judge, will give to me on that day—and not only to me, but also to all who have longed for his appearing.
2 TIMOTHY 4:7-8

Oh, when we turn away from some duty or some fellow-creature, saying that our hearts are too sick and sore with some great yearning of our own, we may often sever the line on which a divine message was coming to us. We shut out the man, and we shut out the angel who had sent him on to open the door. . . There is a plan working in our lives; and if we keep our hearts quiet and our eyes open, it all works together; and, if we don't, it all fights together, and goes on fighting till it comes right, somehow, somewhere.

—ANNIE KEARY

January 17

I consider that our present sufferings are not comparing with the glory that will be revealed in us.
ROMANS 8:18

True courage is about facing life without flinching. I don't mean the times when the right path is hard, but glorious at the end. I'm talking about enduring the boredom, the messiness, and the inconvenience of doing what is right.

—ROBIN HOBB

January 18

Grave on thy heart each past "red-letter day"!
Forget not all the sunshine of the way
By which the Lord hath led thee; answered prayers,
And joys unasked, strange blessings, lifted cares,
Grand promise-echoes! Thus thy life shall be
One record of His love and faithfulness to thee.

F. R. HAVERGAL

Each mistake teaches you something new about yourself. There is no failure, remember, except in no longer trying. It is the courage to continue that counts.

—CHRIS BRADFORD

January 19

Rejoice always.
1 THESSALONIANS 5:16

For God did not give us a spirit of timidity,
but a spirit of power, of love and of self-discipline.
2 TIMOTHY 1:7

We are in 1903 and I am nearly seventy-one years old. I always thought I should love to grow old, and I find it is even more delightful than I thought. It is so delicious to be done with things, and to feel no need any longer to concern myself much about earthly affairs. I seem on the verge of a most delightful journey to a place of unknown joys and pleasures, and things here seem of so little importance compared to things there, that they have lost most of their interest for me. I cannot describe the sort of done-with-the-world feeling I have. It is not that I feel as if I was going to die at all, but simply that the world seems to me nothing but a passageway to the real life beyond; and passage ways are very unimportant places. It is of very little account what sort of things they contain, or how they are furnished. One just hurries through them to get to the place beyond. My wants seem to be gradually narrowing down, my personal wants, I mean, and I often think I could be quite content in the Poor-house! I do not know whether this is piety or old age, or a little of each mixed together, but honestly the world and our life in it does seem of too little account to be worth making the least fuss over, when one has such a magnificent prospect close at hand ahead of one; and I am tremendously content to let one activity after another go, and to await quietly and happily the opening of the door at the end of the passage way, that will let me in to my real abiding place. So you may think of me as happy and contented, surrounded with unnumbered blessings, and delighted to be seventy-one years old.

—MRS. PEARSALL SMITH

January 20

However, as it is written: "no eye has seen, nor ear has heard, no mind has conceived what the God has prepared for those who love him"— but God has revealed it to us by his Spirit.
1 CORINTHIANS 2:9

Send down Thy likeness from above.
And let this my adorning be
Clothe me with wisdom, patience, love,
With lowliness and purity.
JOACHIM LANGE

There is no beautifier of complexion, or form, or behavior, like the wish to scatter joy and not pain around us.

—RALPH WALDO EMERSON

January 21

It is God who arms me with strength
and makes my way perfect.
He makes my feet like the feet of a deer;
he enables me to stand on the heights.
PSALMS 18:32

Thy saints on earth, and those above,
Here join in sweet accord:
One body all in mutual love,
And thou their common Lord.
Yes, thou that body wilt present
Before thy Father's face,
Nor shall a wrinkle or a spot
Its beauteous form disgrace.
ANONYMOUS

Man, by living wholly in submission to the Divine Influence, becomes surrounded with, and creates for himself, internal pleasures infinitely greater than any he can otherwise attain to a state of heavenly Beatitude.

—J. P. GREAVES

January 22

Finally, brothers, whatever is true, whatever is noble, whatever is right, whatever is pure, whatever is lovely, whatever is admirable—if anything is excellent or praiseworthy—think about such things.
PHILIPPIANS 4:8

So relax into life, breathe deep and let go.
Attain what you need but don't sell your soul.
For it's a treasure far beyond the mere baubles of men
and once lost, much harder to earn back again.
MARK RICKERBY

Gratitude means to recognize the good in your life, be thankful for whatever you have, some people may not even have one of those things you consider precious to you. Each day give thanks for the gift of life. You are blessed.

—PABLO

As a prisoner for the Lord, then, I urge you to live a life worthy of the calling you have received. Be completely humble and gentle; be patient, bearing with one another in love. Make every effort to keep the unity of the Spirit through the bond of peace.
EPHESIANS 4:1

> *Bitter your acts, bitter am I,*
> *Kindness your deeds, kindness am I,*
> *Pleasant and gentle, so you are,*
> *Fine honeyed lips and sweet talker.*
> RUMI

Whatever you do, you need courage. Whatever course you decide upon, there is always someone to tell you that you are wrong. There are always difficulties arising that tempt you to believe your critics are right. To map out a course of action and follow it to an end requires some of the same courage that a soldier needs. Peace has its victories, but it takes brave men and women to win them.
—RALPH WALDO EMERSON

I will praise the Lord, who counsels me.
PSALMS 16:7

My father, teach us not only thy will, but how to do it. Teach us the best way of doing the best thing, lest we spoil the end by unworthy means.
REV. J.H. JOWETT

We are all meant to shine, as children do. We were born to make manifest the glory of God that is within us. It's not just in some of us; it's in everyone. And as we let our own light shine, we unconsciously give other people permission to do the same. As we are liberated from our own fear, our presence automatically liberates others. —MARIANNE WILLIAMSON

January 25

Never be lacking in zeal, but keep your spiritual fervor, serving the Lord.
ROMANS 12:11

Anyone then, who knows the good he ought to do and doesn't do it, sins.
JAMES 4:17

*We cannot kindle when we will
The fire that in the heart resides,
The spirit bloweth and is still,*

In mystery our soul abides:
But tasks in hours of insight willed
Can be through hours of gloom fulfilled.
MATTHEW ARNOLD

January 26

Dear friends, now we are children of God,
and what we will be has not yet been made known.
I JOHN 3:2

You have within you, right now, everything you need to deal with
whatever the world can throw at you.
BRIAN TRACY

No star is ever lost we once have seen,
We always may be what we might have been.
Since Good, though only thought, has life and breath,
God's life—can always be redeemed from death
And evil, in its nature, is decay,
And any hour can blot it all away
The hopes that lost in some far distance seem,
May be the truer life, and this the dream.
A. A. PROCTER

For this is what the high and lofty One says—he who lives forever, whose name is holy: I live a high and holy place, but also with him who is contrite and lowly in spirit, to revive the spirit of the lowly and to revive the heart of the contrite.

ISAIAH 57:15

One word
Frees us of all the weight and pain of life:
That word is love.
SOPHOCLES

The greatest happiness of life is the conviction that we are loved—loved for ourselves, or rather, loved in spite of ourselves.

—WILLIAM SHAKESPEARE

There is a sacredness in tears. They are not a mark of weakness, but of power. They speak more eloquently than ten thousand tongues. They are the messengers of overwhelming grief, of deep contrition and of unspeakable love.

—WASHINGTON IRVING

January 28

*You open your hand and satisfy
the desires of every living thing.*
PSALMS 45:16

*What Thou shalt today provide,
Let me as a child receive
What tomorrow may betide,
Calmly to Thy wisdom leave.
'Tis enough that Thou wilt care;
Why should I the burden bear?*
J. NEWTON

Have we found that anxiety about possible consequences increased
the clearness of our judgment, made us wiser and braver in
meeting the present, and arming ourselves for the future? . . . If
we had prayed for this day's bread, and left the next to itself, if
we had not huddled our days together, not allotting to each its
appointed task, but ever deferring that to the future, and drawing
upon the future for its own troubles, which must be met when they
come whether we have anticipated them or not, we should have
found a simplicity and honesty in our lives, a capacity for work, an
enjoyment in it, to which we are now, for the most part, strangers.

—F. D. MAURICE

January 29

*For I am the Lord, your God, who takes hold of your right hand,
and says to you, Do not fear; I will help you.*
ISAIAH 41:13

*Show the wonder of your great love,
you who save by your right hand those who take refuge
in you from their foes.*
PSALMS 17:7

*I Take Thy hand, and fears grow still
Behold Thy face, and doubts remove
Who would not yield his wavering will
To perfect Truth and boundless Love?*
SAMUEL JOHNSON

I learned that courage was not the absence of fear, but the triumph over it. The brave man is not he who does not feel afraid, but he who conquers that fear.

—NELSON MANDELA

January 30

*If I rise on the wings of the dawn,
if I settle on the far side of the sea,
even there your hand will guide me,
your right hand will hold me fast.*
PSALMS 139:9-10

Faith is belief in what you cannot see or prove or touch. Faith is
walking face-first and full-speed into the dark.

—ELIZABETH GILBERT

January 31

*. . . in all your ways acknowledge him,
and he will make your paths straight.*
PROVERBS 3:6

*He makes me lie down in green pastures,
He leads me to still waters. . . .*
PSALMS 23:2

The Shepherd knows what pastures are best for his sheep, and they
must not question nor doubt, but trustingly follow Him. Perhaps
He sees that the best pastures for some of us are to be found in the
midst of opposition or of earthly trials. If He leads you there, you
may be sure they are green for you, and You will grow and be made
strong by feeding there. Perhaps He sees that the best waters for
you to walk beside will be raging waves of trouble and Borrow. If
this should be the case, He will make them still waters for you, and
you must go and lie down beside them, and let them have all their
blessed influences upon you.

—H. W. S.

February

Ye have need of patience, that, after ye have done the will of God,
ye might receive the promise.

HEBREWS 10:36

There is a story of a man who prayed earnestly one morning for grace to overcome his besetting sin of impatience. A little later he missed a train by half a minute and spent an hour stamping up and down the station platform in furious vexation. Five minutes before the next train came in he suddenly realized that here had been the answer to his prayer. He had been given an hour to practice the virtue of patience; he had missed the opportunity and wasted the hour. There are also many stories of men who have similarly, missed trains which have been wrecked, and who ascribe their escape to Providence. If they are combining the thought of God as the celestial chess-player with the thought of God as preeminently concerned in their enjoyment of earthly life at the expense of others, there is not much to be said for their point of view. But if they are humbly acknowledging a call to further service on earth before they pass beyond, they are rightly interpreting their escape. In all probability all the events which led up to all these men missing their various trains could be adequately accounted for in terms of the interaction of natural law, human freedom, and divine grace. But at every point within the interaction God sees what are its possibilities for good, and the man who shares His enlightenment and His power and gives himself to make that good come true, has found the meaning of that moment and his 'special providence'. The gates of the future are indeed open, the universe is in the making. But only if made aright can the making stand. . . .

—LEONARD HODGSON

Defend the cause of the weak and fatherless,
Maintain the rights of the poor and oppressed.
Rescue the weak and needy;
deliver them from the hand of the wicked.
PSALMS 82:3-4

Defend the weak, protect both young and old, never desert
your friends. Give justice to all, be fearless in battle and
always ready to defend the right.
BRIAN JACQUES

The love of our neighbor is the only door out of the dungeon
of self, where we mope and mow, striking sparks, and rubbing
phosphorescence out of the walls, and blowing our own breath in
our own nostrils, instead of issuing to the fair sunlight of God, the
sweet winds of the universe. The man thinks his consciousness
is himself; whereas his life consisteth in the inbreathing of God,
and the consciousness of the universe of truth. To have himself, to
know himself, to enjoy himself, he calls life; whereas, if he would
forget himself, tenfold would be his life in God and his neighbors.
The region of man's life is a spiritual region. God, his friends, his
neighbours, his brothers all, is the wide world in which alone his
spirit can find room. Himself is his dungeon. If he feels it not now,
he will yet feel it one day-feel it as a living soul would feel being
prisoned in a dead body, wrapped in sevenfold cerements, and
buried in a stone-ribbed vault within the last ripple of the sound
of chanting people in the church above. His life is not in knowing
that he lives, but in loving all forms of life. He is made for the All;
for God, who is the All, is his life. And the essential joy of his life
lies abroad in the liberty of the All. His delights, like those of the

Ideal Wisdom, are with the sons of men. His health is in the body of which the Son of Man is the head. The whole region is open to him—nay, he must live in it or perish.

—GEORGE MACDONALD

February 3

Search me, O God, and know my heart;
Test me and know my anxious thoughts.
See if there is any offensive way in me,
and lead me in the way everlasting.
PSALMS 139:23-24

Wilt thou forgive that sinn where I begunn,
Which is my sinn, though it were done before?
Wilt thou forgive those sinns, through which I runn,
And doe them still, though still I doe deplore?
JOHN DONNE

These people fail to realize that it is on the inside that God must be defended, not on the outside. They should direct their anger at themselves. For evil in the open is but evil from within that has been let out. The main battlefield for good is not the open ground of the public arena but the small clearing of each heart.

—YANN MARTEL

February 4

*Do not let any unwholesome talk
come out of your mouths,
but only what is helpful for building
others up according to their needs,
that it may benefit those who listen.*
EPHESIANS 4:29

*Set a guard over my mouth,
O Lord; keep watch over the door of my lips.*
PSALMS 141:4

*Be Impeccable With Your Word:
Speak with integrity. Say only what you mean. Avoid using the
word to speak against yourself or to gossip about others. Use the
power of your word in the direction of truth and love.*
MIGUEL RUIZ

When we remember out temptations to give quick indulgence
to disappointment or irritation or unsympathizing weariness
. . . and how hard a thing it is from day to day to meet our fellow-
men, our neighbors, or even our own households, in all moods,
in all discordances between the world without us and the frames
within . . . with only kindly feeling finding expression and
ungenial feeling at least inwardly imprisoned; we shall be ready
to acknowledge that the man who has thus attained is master of
himself, and in the graciousness of his power is fashioned upon the
style of a Perfect Man.

—J. H. THOM

February 5

Blessed are they who maintain justice,
who constantly do what is right.
PSALMS 106:3

Let my heart the cradle be
Of Thy bleak Nativity!
Tossed by wintry tempests wild,
If it rock Thee, Holy Child,
Then, as grows the outer din,
Greater peace shall reign within.
JOHN BANISTER TABB

You will say that these are very small sins; and doubtless, like all young tempters, you are anxious to be able to report spectacular wickedness. But do remember, the only thing that matters is the extent to which you separate the man from the Enemy. It does not matter how small the sins are provided that their cumulative effect is to edge the man away from the Light and out into the Nothing. Murder is no better than cards if cards can do the trick. Indeed the safest road to Hell is the gradual one-the gentle slope, soft underfoot, without sudden turnings, without milestones, without signposts.

—C.S.LEWIS

February 6

Whoever trusts in the Lord is kept safe.
PROVERBS 29:25

Enter my heart, O Holy Spirit,
come in blessed mercy and set me free.
Throw open, O Lord, the locked doors of my mind;
cleanse the chambers of my thought for thy dwelling:
light there the fires of thine own holy brightness in new
understandings of truth,
O Holy Spirit, very God, whose presence is liberty,
grant me the perfect freedom
to be thy servant
today, tomorrow, evermore.
ERIC MILNER-WHITE

Oh, the comfort—the inexpressible comfort of feeling safe with
a person—having neither to weigh thoughts nor measure words,
but pouring them all right out, just as they are, chaff and grain
together; certain that a faithful hand will take and sift them, keep
what is worth keeping, and then with the breath of kindness blow
the rest away.

—DINAH MARIA MULOCK CRAIK

Aim for perfection, listen to my appeal, be of one mind, live in peace.
And the God of love and peace will be with you.
2 CORINTHIANS 13:11

And oft, when in my heart was heard
Thy timely mandate, I deferred
The task, in smoother walks to stray;
But thee I now would serve more strictly, if I may.
WILLIAM WORDSWORTH

I wanted a perfect ending. Now I've learned, the hard way, that
some poems don't rhyme, and some stories don't have a clear
beginning, middle, and end. Life is about not knowing, having to
change, taking the moment and making the best of it, without
knowing what's going to happen next. Delicious Ambiguity.

—GILDA RADNER

He leadeth me beside the still waters.
He restoreth my soul;
He leadeth me in the paths of righteousness
for His name's sake.
PSALMS 23:2-3

Lead me from death
to Life, from falsehood to Truth

Lead me from despair
to Hope, from fear to Trust

Lead me from hate
to Love, from war to Peace

Let Peace fill our heart,
our world, our universe.
SATISH KUMAR, PRAYER FOR PEACE MOVEMENT

. . . He will guide us in a sure path, though it be a rough one:
though shadows hang upon it, yet He will be with us. He will bring
us home at last. Through much trial it may be, and weariness, in
much fear and fainting of heart, in much sadness and loneliness,
in griefs that the world never knows, and under burdens that the
nearest never suspect. Yet He will suffice for all. By His eye or by
His voice He will guide us, if we be docile and gentle; by His staff
and by His rod, if we wander or are wilful: any how, and by all
means, He will bring us to His rest.

—H. E. MANNING

February 9

Everything is possible for him who believes.
MARK 9:23

Now, God be prais'd, that to believing souls
Gives light in darkness, comfort in despair!
WILLIAM SHAKESPEARE

Five years ago I came to believe in Christ's teaching, and my life suddenly changed; I ceased to desire what I had previously desired, and began to desire what I formerly did not want . . . The direction of my life and my desires became different, and good and evil changed places. . . .

I, like that thief on the cross, have believed Christ's teaching and been saved. And this is no far-fetched comparison, but the closest expression of the condition of spiritual despair and horror at the problem of life and death in which I lived formerly, and of the condition of peace and happiness in which I am now. I, like the thief, knew that I had lived and was living badly. . . . I, like the thief, knew that I was unhappy and suffering . . . I, like the thief to the cross, was nailed by some force to that life of suffering and evil. And as, after the meaningless sufferings and evils of life, the thief awaited the terrible darkness of death, so did I await the same thing.

In all this I was exactly like the thief, but the difference was that the thief was already dying, while I was still living. The thief might believe that his salvation lay there beyond the grave, but I could not be satisfied with that, because besides a life beyond the grave life still awaited me here. But I did not understand that life. It seemed to me terrible. And suddenly I heard the words of Christ and understood them, and life and death ceased to seem to me evil, and instead of despair I experienced happiness and the joy of life undisturbed by death.

—LEO TOLSTOY

Promise Yourself

*To be so strong that nothing
can disturb your peace of mind.
To talk health, happiness, and prosperity
to every person you meet.*

*To make all your friends feel
that there is something in them
To look at the sunny side of everything
and make your optimism come true.*

*To think only the best, to work only for the best,
and to expect only the best.
To be just as enthusiastic about the success of others
as you are about your own.*

*To forget the mistakes of the past
and press on to the greater achievements of the future.
To wear a cheerful countenance at all times
and give every living creature you meet a smile.*

*To give so much time to the improvement of yourself
that you have no time to criticize others.
To be too large for worry, too noble for anger, too strong for fear,
and too happy to permit the presence of trouble.*

*To think well of yourself and to proclaim this fact to the world,
not in loud words but great deeds.
To live in faith that the whole world is on your side*

so long as you are true to the best that is in you.
CHRISTIAN D. LARSON

O give us patience and steadfastness in adversity, strengthen our weakness, comfort us in trouble and distress, help us to fight; grant unto us that in true obedience and contentation of mind we may give over our own wills unto thee our Father in all things, according to the example of they beloved Son, that in adversity we grudge not, but offer up ourselves unto thee without contradiction . . . O give us a willing and cheerful mind, that we may gladly suffer and bear all things for thy sake.

—BISHOP MILES COVERDALE

February 11

---

*Then his disciples said to each other,
"Could someone have brought him food?"*

*"My food," said Jesus,
"is to do the will of him who sent me and to finish his work."*
JOHN 4:33-34

*He who God's will has borne and done,
And his own restless longings tilled;
What else he does, or has foregone,
His mission he has well fulfilled.*
ANONYMOUS

If a man is called to be a streetsweeper, he should sweep streets
even as Michelangelo painted, or Beethoven played music, or
Shakespeare wrote poetry. He should sweep streets so well that all
the hosts of heaven and earth will pause to say, here lived a great
streetsweeper who did his job well.

—MARTIN LUTHER KING, JR.

February 12

*All this is for your benefit, so that the grace that is reaching more and
more people may cause thanksgiving to overflow to the glory of God.*
2 CORINTHIANS 4:15

For even the purest delight may pall,
And power must fail, and the pride must fall,
And the love of the dearest friends grow small—
But the glory of the Lord is all in all.
R. D. BLACKMORE

"Dear God," she prayed, "let me be something every minute of
every hour of my life. Let me be gay; let me be sad. Let me be cold;
let me be warm. Let me be hungry...have too much to eat. Let me
be ragged or well dressed. Let me be sincere, be deceitful. Let me be
truthful; let me be a liar. Let me be honorable and let me sin. Only
let me be something every blessed minute. And when I sleep, let
me dream all the time so that not one little piece of living is ever
lost."

—BETTY SMITH

Yet not as I will, but as you will.
MATTHEW 26:39

*. . . your kingdom come, your will be done,
on earth as it is in heaven.*
MATTHEW 6:10

Do everyday or two something for no other reason than that you would rather not do it, so that when the hour of dire need draws nigh, it may find you not unnerved and untrained to stand the test. . . .

—WILLIAM JAMES

Dare to look up to God, and say, "Make use of me for the future as Thou wilt. I am of the same mind; I am one with Thee. I refuse nothing which seems good to Thee. Lead me whither Thou wilt, clothe me in whatever dress Thou wilt. Is it Thy will that I should be in a public or a private condition, dwell here, or be banished, be poor or rich? Under all these circumstances, I will testify unto Thee before men."

—EPICTETUS

I would like you to be free from concern.
1 CORINTHIANS 7:32

O LORD, how happy should we be
If we could cast our care on Thee,
If we from self could rest;
And feel at heart that One above,
In perfect wisdom, perfect love,
Is working for the best.
J. ANSTICE

Cast all thy care on God. See that all thy cares be such as thou canst cast on God, and then hold none back. Never brood over thyself; never stop short in thyself; but cast thy whole self, even this very care which distresseth thee, upon God. Be not anxious about little things, if thou wouldst learn to trust God with thine all. Act upon faith in little things; commit thy daily cares and anxieties to Him; and He will strengthen thy faith for any greater trials. Rather, give thy whole self into God's hands and so trust Him to take care of thee in all lesser things, as being His, for His own sake, whose thou art.

—E. B. PUSEY

Finally, all of you, live in harmony with one another,
be sympathetic, love as brothers . . .
1 PETER 3:8

The world is my country,
all mankind are my brethren,
and to do good is my religion.

THOMAS PAINE

There is only one way of following Jesus and of worshipping
God, and that is to be reconciled with our brethren. If we come
to hear the word of God and receive the sacrament without first
being reconciled with our neighbours, we shall come to our own
damnation. In the sight of God we are murderers. Therefore "go
thy way, first be reconciled with thy brother, and then come and
offer thy gift." This is a hard way, but it is the way Jesus requires
if we are to follow Him. It is a way which brings much personal
humiliation and insult, but it is indeed the way to Him, our
crucified Brother, and therefore a way of grace abounding. In Jesus
the service of God and the service of the least of the brethren were
one. He went His way and became reconciled with His brother and
offered Himself as the one true sacrifice to His Father.

We are still living in the age of grace, for each of us still has a
brother, we are still "with him in the way." The court of judgement
lies ahead, and there is still a chance for us to be reconciled with
our brother and pay our debt to him. The hour is coming when
we shall meet the judge face to face, and then it will be too late.
We shall then receive our sentence and be made to pay the last
farthing. But do we realize that at this point our brother comes
to us in the guise not of law, but of grace? It is grace that we are
allowed to find favour with our brother, and pay our debt to him; it
is grace that we are allowed to become reconciled with him. In our
brother we find grace before the seat of judgement.

Only He can speak thus to us, who as our Brother has Himself
become our grace, our atonement, our deliverance from judgement.

The humanity of the Son of God empowers us to find favour with our brother. May the disciples of Jesus think upon this grace aright!

—DIETRICH BONHOEFFER

February 16

. . . to love the Lord your God and to serve
him with all your heart and with all your soul . . .
DEUTERONOMY 11:13

And you, my son Solomon,
acknowledge the God of your father,
and serve him with wholehearted devotion and
with a willing mind. . .
1 CHRONICLES 28:9

My spirit bare before Thee stands;
I bring no gift, I ask no sign,
I come to Thee with empty hands,
the surer to be filled from Thine.
DORA GREENWELL

Little things come daily, hourly, within our reach, and they are
not less calculated to set forward our growth in holiness, than are
the greater occasions which occur but rarely. Moreover, fidelity in
trifles, and an earnest seeking to please God in little matters, is a
test of real devotion and love. Let your aim be to please our dear
Lord perfectly in little things, and to attain a spirit of childlike
simplicity and dependence. In proportion as self-love and self-
confidence are weakened, and our will bowed to that of God,
so will hindrances disappear, the internal troubles and contests
which harassed the soul vanish, and it will be filled with peace and
tranquility.

—JEAN NICOLAS GROU

February 17

Blessed is the man who perseveres under trial,
because when he has stood the test,
he will receive the crown of life that God
has promised to those who love him.
JAMES 1:12

In the bitter waves of woe,
Beaten and tossed about
By the sullen winds that blow
From the desolate shores of doubt,
Where the anchors that faith has cast
Are dragging in the gale,
I am quietly holding fast
To the things that cannot fail.
WASHINGTON GLADDEN

A friend is a possession we earn, not a gift. . . .The Lord has
declared that those who serve him and keep his commandments
are called his servants. After they have been tested and tried
and are found faithful and true in all things, they are called no
longer servants, but friends. His friends are the ones he will take
into his kingdom and with whom he will associate in an eternal
inheritance.

—MARVIN J. ASHTON

<hr />

February 18

*In this you greatly rejoice, though now for a little while you may have
had to suffer grief in all kinds of trials. These have come so that your
faith— of greater worth than gold . . . may be proved genuine and
may result in praise, glory and honor when Jesus Christ is revealed.*
1 PETER 1:6-7

*There are people in the world so hungry, that God cannot appear to
them except in the form of bread.*
MAHATMA GANDHI

There is no moment at which God does not present Himself under
the guise of some suffering, some consolation, or some duty.
All that occurs within us, around us, and by our means covers
and hides His divine action. His action is there, most really and
certainly present, but in an invisible manner, the result of which
is that we are always being taken by surprise and that we only
recognize His action after it has passed away. Could we pierce
the veil, and were we vigilant and attentive, God would reveal

Himself continuously to us and we should rejoice in His action in everything that happened to us.

—J. P. DE CAUSSADE

February 19

Teach me to do your will, for you are my God;
may your good Spirit lead me on level ground.
PSALMS 143:10

Do not merely listen to the word and so deceive yourselves.
Do what it says.
Anyone who listens to the word but does not do what it says
is like a man who looks at his face in a mirror
and after looking at himself, goes away and
immediately forgets what he looks like.
But the man who looks intently into the perfect law
that gives freedom, and continues to do this,
not forgetting what he has heard, but doing it
—he will be blessed in what he does.
JAMES 1:22

Cheered by the presence of God, I will do at each moment, without anxiety, according to the strength which He shall give me, the work that His Providence assigns me. I will leave the rest without concern; it is not my affair. I ought to consider the duty to which I am called each day, as the work that God has given me to do, and to apply myself to it in a manner worthy of His glory, that is to say, with exactness and in peace. I must neglect nothing; I must be violent about nothing.

—FENELON

Therefore let us stop passing judgement on one another.
Instead, make up your mind not to put any stumbling block or
obstacle in your brother's way.
ROMANS 14:13

If you judge people, you have no time to love them.
MOTHER THERESA

A vexation arises, and our expressions of impatience hinder others
from taking it patiently. Disappointment, ailment, or even weather
depresses us; and our look or tone of depression hinders others
from maintaining a cheerful and thankful spirit. We say an unkind
thing and another is hindered in learning the holy lesson of charity
that thinketh no evil. We say a provoking thing, and our sister
or brother is hindered in that day's effort to be meek. How sadly,
too, we may hinder without word or act! For wrong feeling is more
infectious than wrong doing; especially the various phases of ill
temper—gloominess, touchiness, discontent, irritability—do we
not know how catching these are?

—F. R. HAVERGAL

February 21

Which of you, if his son asks for bread, will give him a stone? Or if he asks for a fish, will give him a snake? If you, then, though you are evil, know how to give good gifts to your children, how much more will your Father in heaven give good gifts to those who ask him!

MATTHEW 7:9-11

For His great love has compassed
Our nature, and our need
We know not; but He knoweth,
And He will bless indeed.
Therefore, O heavenly Father,
Give what is best to me
And take the wants unanswered,
As offerings made to Thee.

ANONYMOUS

If the world were merely seductive, that would be easy. If it were merely challenging, that would be no problem. But I arise in the morning torn between a desire to improve the world and a desire to enjoy the world. This makes it hard to plan the day.

—E.B. WHITE

And when you pray, do not be like the hypocrites, for they love to pray standing in the synagogues and on the street corners to be seen by men. . . . But when you pray, go into your room, close the door and pray to your Father, who is unseen. Then your Father, who sees what is done in secret, will reward you.

MATTHEW 6:5-6

We breathe our secret wish,
The importunate longing which no man may see;
We ask it humbly, or, more restful still,
We leave it all to Thee.

SUSAN COOLIDGE

I pray because I can't help myself. I pray because I'm helpless. I pray because the need flows out of me all the time—waking and sleeping. It doesn't change God—it changes me.

—WILLIAM NICHOLSON

Be strong and take heart, all you who hope in the Lord.
PSALMS 31:24

Promise me you'll always remember: You're braver than you believe, and stronger than you seem, and smarter than you think.
A. A. MILNE

There is neither happiness nor misery in the world; there is only the comparison of one state with another, nothing more. He who has felt the deepest grief is best able to experience supreme happiness. We must of felt what it is to die, Morrel, that we may appreciate the enjoyments of life.

Live, then, and be happy, beloved children of my heart, and never forget, that until the day God will deign to reveal the future to man, all human wisdom is contained in these two words, "Wait and Hope."

—ALEXANDRE DUMAS

February 24

---

*I have told you these things,
so that in me you may have peace.*
JOHN 16:33

Peace flows into me
As the tide to the pool by the shore;
It is mine forevermore,
It ebbs not back like the sea.

I am the pool of blue
That worships the vivid sky;
My hopes were heaven-high,
They are all fulfilled in you.

I am the pool of gold
When sunset burns and dies—
You are my deepening skies,
Give me your stars to hold.
SARA TEASDALE

Accustom yourself to unreasonableness and injustice. Abide in peace in the presence of God, who sees all these evils more clearly than you do, and who permits them. Be content with doing with calmness the little which depends upon yourself, and let all else be to you as if it were not.

—FENELON

February 25

But now this is what the Lord says—he who created you, O Jacob, he who formed you, O Israel: "Fear not, for I have redeemed you; I have summoned you by name; you are mine."

ISAIAH 43:1

Thou art as much His care as if beside
Nor man nor angel lived in heaven or earth;
Thus sunbeams pour alike their glorious tide,
To light up worlds, or wake an insect's mirth.

J. KEBLE

When I first found out I had cancer, I didn't know what to pray for. I didn't know if I should pray for healing or life or death. Then I found peace in praying for what my folks call, 'God's perfect will.' As it evolved, my prayer has become, 'Lord, let me live until I die.' By that I mean I want to live, love, and serve fully until death comes. If that prayer is answered, how long really doesn't matter. Whether it's just a few months or a few years is really immaterial.

—SISTER THEA BOWMAN

February 26

The Lord is near to all who call on him . . .
PSALMS 145:18

I love the Lord, for he heard my voice;
he heard my cry for mercy.
Because he turned his ear to me,
I will call on him as long as I live.
PSALMS 116:1-2

Take courage, and turn your troubles, which are without remedy, into material for spiritual progress. Often turn to our Lord, who is watching you, poor frail little being as you are, amid your labors and distractions. He sends you help, and blesses your affliction. This thought should enable you to bear your troubles patiently and gently, for love of Him who only allows you to be tried for your own good. Raise your heart continually to God, seek His aid, and let the foundation stone of your consolation be your happiness in being His. All vexations and annoyances will be comparatively unimportant while you know that you have such a Friend, such a Stay, such a Refuge. May God be ever in your heart.

—ST. FRANCIS DE SALES

February 27

But blessed is the man who trusts in the Lord,
whose confidence is in him.
JEREMIAH 17:27

Trust in the Lord and do good;
dwell in the land and enjoy safe pasture.
PSALMS 37:3

Build a little fence of trust
Around to-day;
Fill the space with loving work,
And therein stay;
Look not through the sheltering bars
Upon to-morrow,
God will help thee bear what comes,
Of joy or sorrow.
MARY FRANCES BUTTS

Often the answer to our prayer does not come while we're on our
knees but while we're on our feet serving the Lord and serving
those around us. Selfless acts of service and consecration refine
our spirits remove the scales from our spiritual eyes and open the
windows of heaven. By becoming the answer to someone's prayer
we often find the answer to our own.

—DIETER F. USHTDORF

February 28

Dear friends, let us love one another, for love comes from God.
Everyone who loves has been born of God and knows God.

1 JOHN 4:7

I will tell you the truth, whatever you did for one of the least
of these brothers of mine, you did for me.

MATTHEW 26:40

Then next, to love our brethren that were made
Of that self mould, and that self Maker's hand . . .
That we, and to the same again shall fade,
Where they shall have like heritage of land,
However here on higher steps we stand;
Which also were with self-same price redeemed
That we, however of us light esteemed.

And were they not, yet since that loving Lord
Commanded us to love them for His sake,
Even for His sake, and for His sacred word,
Which in His last bequest He to us spake,
We should them love, and with their needs partake;
Knowing that whatso'er to them we give,
We give to Him by whom we all do live.

EDMUND SPENSER

Love is what we are born with. Fear is what we learn. The spiritual
journey is the unlearning of fear and prejudices and the acceptance
of love back in our hearts. Love is the essential reality and our

purpose on earth. To be consciously aware of it, to experience love in ourselves and others, is the meaning of life. Meaning does not lie in things. Meaning lies in us.

—MARIANNE WILLIAMSON

February 29

But for you who revere my name, the sun of righteousness will rise with healing in its wings.
MALACHI 4:2

Heal me, O Lord, and I will be healed.
JEREMIAH 17:14

We tell Thee of our care,
Of the sore burden, pressing day by day,
And in the light and pity of Thy face,
The burden melts away.
SUSAN COOLIDGE

When we honestly ask ourselves which person in our lives mean the most to us, we often find that it is those who, instead of giving advice, solutions, or cures, have chosen rather to share our pain and touch our wounds with a warm and tender hand. The friend who can be silent with us in a moment of despair or confusion, who can stay with us in an hour of grief and bereavement, who can tolerate not knowing, not curing, not healing and face with us the reality of our powerlessness, that is a friend who cares.

—HENRI J.M. NOUWEN

Give me strength to be the first to tender the healing word and the renewal of friendship, that the bonds of amity and the flow of charity may be strengthened for the good of the brethren and the furthering of thine eternal, loving purpose.

—CECIL HUNT

March

March 1

Never again will they hunger; never again will they thirst.
REVELATIONS 7:16

Every good and perfect gift is from above . . .
JAMES 1:17

O have decided to stick to love—
Hate is too great a burden to bear.
MARTIN LUTHER KING, JR.

It has been well said that no man ever sank under the burden of
the day. It is when to-morrow's burden is added to the burden of
today that the weight is more than a man can bear. Never load
yourselves so, my friends. If you find yourselves so loaded, at least
remember this: it is your own doing, not God's. He begs you to
leave the future to Him, and mind the present.

—GEORGE MACDONALD

March 2

This is the message you heard from the beginning:
We should love one another.
1 JOHN 3:11

Being deeply loved by someone gives you strength,
while loving someone deeply gives you courage.
LAO TZU

> *So to the calmly gathered thought*
> *The innermost of life is taught,*
> *The mystery, dimly understood,*
> *That love of God is love of good;*
> *That to be saved is only this—*
> *Salvation from our selfishness.*

J. G. WHITTER

Love is that condition in the human spirit so profound that it empowers us to develop courage; to trust that courage and build bridges with it; to trust those bridges and cross over them so we can attempt to reach each other.

—MAYA ANGELOU

March 3

Why, you do not even know what will happen tomorrow. . . . you ought to say, "If it is the Lord's will, we will live and do this or that."

JAMES 4:14

> *"Lie still, be strong, today: but, Lord, tomorrow,*
> *What of tomorrow, Lord?*
> *Shall there be rest from toil, be truce from sorrow,*
> *Be living green upon the sward,*
> *Now but a barren grave to me, Be joy for sorrow?"*
>
> *'Did I not die for thee?*
> *Do I not live for thee? Leave me tomorrow.'*

CHRISTINA G. ROSSETTI

Life can be long or short, it all depends on how you choose to live it. It's like forever, always changing. For any of us our forever could end in an hour, or a hundred years from now. You can never know for sure, so you'd better make every second count. What you have to decide is how you want your life to be. If your forever was ending tomorrow, is this how you'd want to have spent it?

—SARAH DESSEN

March 4

To him who overcomes, I will give the right to sit with me on my throne, just as I overcame and sat down with my Father on his throne.
REVELATIONS 3:21

When the night has been too lonely
And the road has been too long,
And you think that love is only
For the lucky and the strong,
Just remember in the winter
Far beneath the bitter snows
Lies the seed that with the sun's love
In the spring becomes the rose.
AMANDA MCBROOM

I count him braver who overcomes his desires than him who conquers his enemies, for the hardest victory is over self.

—ARISTOTLE

March 5

And so after waiting patiently,
Abraham received what was promised.
HEBREWS 6:15

> *Now, Lord, what wait I for*
> *On Thee alone*
> *My hope is all rested,—*
> *Lord, seal me Thine own!*
> *Only Thine own to be,*
> *Only to live to Thee.*
> *Thine, with each day begun,*
> *Thine, with each set of sun,*
> *Thine, till my work is done.*
> ANNA WARNER

We always used to think it was one of the elementary rights of man that he should be able to plan his life in advance, both private life and professional. That is a thing of the past. The pressure of events is forcing us to give up "being anxious for the morrow." But it makes all the difference in the world whether we accept this willingly and in faith (which is what the Sermon on the Mount means) or under compulsion. For most people not to plan for the future means to live irresponsibly and frivolously, to live just for the moment, while some few continue to dream of better times to come. But we cannot take either of these courses. We are still left with only the narrow way, a way often hardly to be found, of living every day as if it were our last, yet in faith and responsibility living as though a splendid future still lay before us. "Houses and fields and vineyards shall yet again be bought in this land," cries Jeremiah as the Holy City is about to be destroyed, a striking contrast to his previous prophecies of woe. It is a divine sign and pledge of better things to come, just when all seems blackest. Thinking and acting for the sake of the coming generation, but taking each day as it comes without fear and anxiety that is the spirit in which we are being forced to live in practice. It is not easy to be brave and hold out, but it is imperative.

—DIETRICH BONHOEFFER

March 6

The Lord is my rock, my fortress and my deliverer;
my God is my rock, in whom I take refuge.
PSALMS 18:2

Be Thou, O Rock of Ages, nigh!
So shall each murmuring thought be gone;
And grief and fear and care shall fly,
As clouds before the mid-day sun.
C. WESLEY

Our whole trouble in our lot in this world rises from the disagreement of our mind therewith. Let the mind be brought to the lot, and the whole tumult is instantly hushed; let it be kept in that disposition, and the man shall stand at ease, in his affliction, like a rock unmoved with waters beating upon it.

—T. BOSTON

There are different kinds of working,
but the same God works all of them in all men.
1 CORINTHIANS 12:6

Confront the dark parts of yourself, and work to banish them
with illumination and forgiveness. Your willingness to wrestle
with your demons will cause your angels to sing.

—AUGUST WILSON

Work, and thou wilt bless the day
Ere the toil be done;
They that work not, can not pray,
Cannot feel the sun.
God is living, working still,
All things work and move;
Work, or lose the power to will,
Lose the power to love.
JOHN SULLIVAN DWIGHT

Let us not become weary in doing good,
for at the proper time we will reap
a harvest if we do not give up.
Therefore as we have opportunity,
let us do good . . .
GALATIANS 6:9-10

The task Thy wisdom hath assigned,
Oh, let me cheerfully fulfil;
In all my works Thy presence find,
And prove Thine acceptable will.
C. WESLEY

It cannot be thought that God sends events to a living soul in order that the soul may be simply passive under the events. If God sends you an event, it must have a meaning; it must be a sign to you that you are to do something, to brace yourself up to some action or to some state of feeling. All that God sends to a human spirit must be significant. God has sent us His Word. We know that He designs us not simply to hear it, but to embrace it with a living faith and a loving obedience. We are to meditate upon it, to apply it to our consciences, mould our character and conduct in conformity to it. Now the same God who has sent us His Word equally sends us the daily occurrences of life, the chief difference being that, whereas the Word has a general voice for all, in which each is to find his own case represented, the occurrences are charged with a more specific message to individuals. Now there is many a man who says, "I will conform myself to the general indication of God's will made to me by His Word"; comparatively few who say, "I will conform myself to the special indications of God's will made to me by His Providence." But why so few? Does not God come home to us more closely, more searchingly, more personally by His Providence than even by His Word? Does not His finger rest upon each of us more particularly in the government of affairs than even in revelation? And why are we to imagine, as many seem to imagine, that no other events but such as are afflictive and calamitous have a voice for us? Why not every event? Why is not the ordinary intercourse of life to be regarded as furnishing in God's design and intention opportunities of either doing or receiving good?

—EDWARD MEYRICK GOULBURN

March 9

. . . and you are to rejoice before the Lord your God in everything you put your hand to.
DEUTERONOMY 12:18

You have it easily in your power to increase the sum total of this world's happiness now. How? By giving a few words of sincere appreciation to someone who is lonely or discouraged. Perhaps you will forget tomorrow the kind words you say today, but the recipient may cherish them over a lifetime.

—DALE CARNEGIE

March 10

God is our refuge and strength, an ever-present help in trouble.
Therefore we will not fear, though the earth give way
and the mountains fall into the heart of the of the sea,
though its waters roar and foam
and the mountains quake with their surging.

PSALMS 46:1-3

Let me do my work each day;
And if the darkened hours of despair overcome me,
May I not forget the strength that comforted me
In the desolation of other times.
May I still remember the bright hours that found me
Walking over the silent hills of my childhood,
Or dreaming on the margin of the quiet river,
When a light glowed within me,
And I promised my early God to have courage
Amid the tempests of the changing years. . . .
MAX EHRMANN

March 11

---

*Cast your cares on the Lord and
he will sustain you; he will never let the righteous fall.*
PSALMS 55:22

When we honestly ask ourselves which person in our lives mean
the most to us, we often find that it is those who, instead of giving
advice, solutions, or cures, have chosen rather to share our pain
and touch our wounds with a warm and tender hand. The friend
who can be silent with us in a moment of despair or confusion,
who can stay with us in an hour of grief and bereavement, who can
tolerate not knowing, not curing, not healing and face with us the
reality of our powerlessness, that is a friend who cares.

— HENRI J.M. NOUWEN

March 12

---

*The Lord bless you and keep you;
the Lord make his face shine upon you
and be gracious to you;
the Lord turn his face toward you and give you peace.*
NUMBERS 6:24-26

I am serene because I know thou lovest me. Because thou lovest me, naught can move me from my peace. Because thou lovest me, I am as one to whom all good has come.

—GAELIC PRAYER

Drop thy still dews of quietness,
Till all our strivings cease;
Take from our souls the strain and stress,
And let our ordered lives confess
The beauty of thy peace.
J. G. WHITTIER

March 13

Your beauty should not come from outward adornment . . . Instead, it should be that of your inner self, the unfading beauty of a gentle and quiet spirit, which is of great worth in God's sight.
1 PETER 3:3-4

The power of finding beauty in the humblest things makes home happy and life lovely.
LOUISA MAY ALCOTT

The truth of a thing, then, is the blossom of it, the thing it is made for, the topmost stone set on with rejoicing; truth in a man's imagination is the power to recognize this truth of a thing; and wherever, in anything that God has made, in the glory of it, be it sky or flower or human face, we see the glory of God, there a true imagination is beholding a truth of God.

—GEORGE MACDONALD

March 14

I call on you, O God, for you will answer me,
give ear to me and hear my prayer.
PSALMS 17:6

Trouble and perplexity drive us to prayer, and prayer driveth away trouble and perplexity.

—P. MELANCHTHON

I choose gentleness. . . Nothing is won by force. I choose to be gentle. If I raise my voice may it be only in praise. If I clench my fist, may it be only in prayer. If I make a demand, may it be only of myself.

—MAX LUCADO

March 15

May your unfailing love be my comfort . . .
PSALMS 119:76

Happiness doesn't lie in conspicuous consumption and the relentless amassing of useless crap. Happiness lies in the person sitting beside you and your ability to talk to them. Happiness is clear-headed human interaction and empathy. Happiness is home. And home is not a house—home is a mythological conceit. It is a state of mind. A place of communion and unconditional love. It is where, when you cross its threshold, you finally feel at peace.

—DENNIS LEHANE

March 16

So whether you eat or drink or whatever you do,
do it all for the glory of God.
1 CORINTHIANS 11:31

If any one would tell you the shortest, surest way to all happiness and all perfection, he must tell you to make it a rule to yourself to thank and praise God for everything that happens to you. For it is certain that whatever seeming calamity happens to you, if you thank and praise God for it, you turn it into a blessing. Could you, therefore, work miracles, you could not do more for yourself than by this thankful spirit; for it heals with a word speaking, and turns all that it touches into happiness.

—WILLIAM LAW

March 17

But as for you, continue in what you have learned and have become convinced of, because you know from whom you learned it . . .
2 TIMOTHY 3:14

For the ear tests words as the tongue tastes food. Let us discern for ourselves what is right; let us learn together what is good.
JOB 34:3-4

What have I learnt where'er I've been,
From all I've heard, from all I've seen?
What know I more that's worth the knowing?
What have I done that's worth the doing?
What have I sought that I should shun?
What duties have I left undone?
PYTHAGORAS

Religion begins in knowledge, proceeds in practice, and ends in happiness.

—BENJAMIN WHICHCOTE

March 18

How good and pleasant it is when brothers live together in unity!
PSALMS 133:1

*Carry each other's burdens,
and in this way you will fulfill the law of Christ.*
GALATIANS 6:2

Make us of one heart and mind;
Courteous, pitiful, and kind;
Lowly, meek, in thought and word,
Altogether like our Lord.

C. WESLEY

Kindly words, sympathizing attentions, watchfulness against wounding men's sensitiveness—these cost very little, but they are priceless in their value.

—F. W. ROBERTSON

March 19

. . . if we are faithless, he will remain faithful,
for he cannot disown himself.

2 TIMOTHY 2:13

Love lives beyond
The tomb, the earth, which fades like dew.
I love the fond,
The faithful, and the true
Love lives in sleep,
The happiness of healthy dreams
Eve's dews may weep,
But love delightful seems.
'Tis heard in Spring
When light and sunbeams, warm and kind,
On angels' wing
Bring love and music to the mind.
And where is voice,
So young, so beautiful and sweet
As nature's choice,

Where Spring and lovers meet?
Love lives beyond
The tomb, the earth, the flowers, and dew.
I love the fond,
The faithful, young and true.
JOHN CLARE

Wisdom comes . . . not from trying to do great things for God . . .
but more from being faithful to the small, obscure tasks few people
ever see.

—CHARLES R. SWINDOLL

March 20

Worship the Lord your God, and serve him only.
MATTHEW 4:10

I've been a great deal happier since I have given up thinking
about what is easy and pleasant, and being discontented because
I couldn't have my own will. Our life is determined for us; and it
makes the mind very free when we give up wishing, and only think
of bearing what is laid upon us, and doing what is given us to do.

—GEORGE ELIOT

March 21

. . . for your Father knows what you need before you ask him.
MATTHEW 6:8

All as God wills, who wisely heeds
To give or to withhold;
And knoweth more of all my needs
Than all my prayers have told.
J. G. WHITTIER

Life moves on, whether we act as cowards or heroes. Life has no other discipline to impose, if we would but realize it, than to accept life unquestioningly. Everything we shut our eyes to, everything we run away from, everything we deny, denigrate or despise, serves to defeat us in the end. What seems nasty, painful, evil, can become a source of beauty, joy, and strength, if faced with an open mind. Every moment is a golden one for him who has the vision to recognize it as such.

—HENRY MILLER

March 22

Well done, good and faithful servant! You have been faithful with a few things; I will put you in charge of many things.
MATTHEW 25:21

There is another very safe and simple way of escape when the dull mood begins to gather round one, and that is to, turn as promptly and as strenuously as one can to whatever work one can at the moment do. If the energy, the clearness, the power of intention, is flagging in us, if we cannot do our best work, still let us do what we can-for we can always do something; if not high work, then low work; if not vivid and spiritual work, then the plain, needful drudgery.

When it is dull and cold and weary weather with us, when the light is hidden, and the mists are thick, and the sleet begins to fall, still we may get on with the work which can be done as well in the dark days as in the bright; work which otherwise will have to be hurried through in the sunshine, taking up its happiest and most fruitful hours. When we seem poorest and least spiritual, when the glow of thankfulness seems to have died quite away, at least we can go on with the comparatively featureless bits of work, the business letters, the mechanism of life, the tasks which may be almost as well done then as ever. And not only, as men have found and said in every age, is the activity itself a safeguard for the time, but also very often, I think, the plainer work is the best way of getting back into the light and warmth that are needed for the higher.

—FRANCIS PAGET

March 23

I can do everything through him who gives me strength.
PHILLIPPIANS 4:13

Strive thou with studious care to find
Some good thy hands may do;
Some way to serve and bless mankind,
Console the heart, relieve the mind,
And open comforts new.
ANONYMOUS

Human felicity is produced not so much by great pieces of good fortune that seldom happen, as by little advantages that occur every day. When men are employed, they are best contented; for on the days they worked they were good-natured and cheerful, and, with the consciousness of having done a good day's work, they spent the evening jollily; but on our idle days they were mutinous and quarrelsome.

—BENJAMIN FRANKLIN

March 24

*I will lie down and sleep in peace, for you alone,
O Lord, make me dwell in safety.*
PSALMS 4:8

If you have a problem that can be fixed, then there is no use in worrying. If you have a problem that cannot be fixed, then there is no use in worrying.

BUDDHIST PROVERB

One evening when Luther saw a little bird perched on a tree, to roost there for the night, he said, "This little bird has had its supper, and now it is getting ready to go to sleep here, quite secure and content, never troubling itself what its food will be, or where its lodging on the morrow. Like David, it 'abides under the shadow of the Almighty.' It sits on its little twig content, and lets God take care."

—ANONYMOUS

March 25

---

*I will listen to what God the Lord will say;
he promises peace to his people . . .*

PSALMS 85:8

*Beyond a wholesome discipline,
be gentle with yourself.
You are a child of the universe
no less than the trees and the stars;
you have a right to be here.
And whether or not it is clear to you,
no doubt the universe is unfolding as it should.
Therefore, be at peace with God,
whatever you conceive Him to be.
And whatever your labors and aspirations,*

in the noisy confusion of life,
keep peace in your soul.
With all its sham,
drudgery, and broken dreams,
it is still a beautiful world.
Be cheerful.
Strive to be happy.

MAX EHRMANN

Speak, Lord, for thy servant heareth. Grant us ears to hear, eyes to see, wills to obey, hearts to love; then declare what thou wilt, reveal what thou wilt, command what thou wilt, demand what thou wilt—Amen.

—CHRISTINA G. ROSSETTI

March 26

Think how you have instructed many, how you have strengthened feeble hands. Your words have supported those who stumbled; you have strengthened faltering knees.

JOB 4:3-4

May I reach
That purest heaven, be to other souls
The cup of strength in some great agony,
Enkindle generous ardor, feed pure love,
Be the sweet presence of a good diffused,
And in diffusion ever more intense!
So shall I join the choir invisible
Whose music is the gladness of the world.

GEORGE ELIOT

Hence we perceive that the true motive for our striving to set ourselves free is to manifest our freedom by resigning it through an act to be renewed every moment, ever resuming and ever resigning it; to the end that our service may be entire, that the service of the hands may likewise be the service of the will; even as the Apostle, being free from all, made himself servant to all. This is the accomplishment of the great Christian paradox, "Whosoever will be great, let him be a minister; and whosoever will be chief, let him be a servant."

—J. C. AND AUGUSTUS HARE

March 27

. . . if we love one another,
God lives in us and his love is made complete in us.
1 JOHN 4:12

God is love.
Whoever lives in love lives in God,
and God in him.
1 JOHN 4:16

O Lord give me strength to refrain from the unkind silence that is born of hardness of heart;the unkind silence that clouds the serenity of understanding and is the enemy of peace. Give me strength to be the first to tender the healing word and the renewal of friendship, that the bonds of amity and the flow of charity may be strengthened for the good of the brethren and the furthering of thine eternal, loving purpose.

—CECIL HUNT

March 28

*I will give thanks to the Lord because of his righteousness
and will sing praise to the name of the Lord Most High.*
PSALMS 7:17

*So am I as the rich, whose blessed key
Can bring him to his sweet up-locked treasure,
The which he will not every hour survey,
For blunting the fine point of seldom pleasure.
Therefore are feasts so solemn and so rare,
Since, seldom coming, in that long year set,
Like stones of worth they thinly placed are,
Or captain jewels in the carconet.
So is the time that keeps you as my chest,
Or as the wardrobe which the robe doth hide,
To make some special instant special blest
By new unfolding his imprison'd pride.
Blessed are you, whose worthiness gives scope,
Being had, to triumph; being lack'd, to hoped.*

SHAKESPEARE

When we lose one blessing, another is often most unexpectedly
given in its place.

—C.S. LEWIS

I will fear no evil, for you are with me . . .
PSALMS 23:4

No coward soul is mine,
No trembler in the world's storm-troubled sphere:
I see Heaven's glories shine,
And faith shines equal, arming me from fear.
EMILY BRONTE

Be like the promontory, against which the waves continually break; but it stands firm, and tames the fury of the water around it. Unhappy am I, because this has happened to me? Not so, but happy am I, though this has happened to me, because I continue free from pain, neither crushed by the present, nor fearing the future. Will then this which has happened prevent thee from being just, magnanimous, temperate, prudent, secure against inconsiderate opinions and falsehood? Remember, too, on every occasion which leads thee to vexation to apply this principle: that this is not a misfortune, but that to bear it nobly is good fortune.

—MARCUS ANTONINUS

You will be secure, because there is hope;
you will look about you and take your rest in safety.
JOB 11:18

Go forth to meet the solemnities and to conquer the trials of existence, believing in a Shepherd of your souls. Then faith in Him will support you in duty, and duty firmly done will strengthen faith; till at last, when all is over here, and the noise and strife of the earthly battle fades upon your dying ear, and you hear, instead thereof, the deep and musical sound of the ocean of eternity, and see the lights of heaven shining on its waters still and fair in their radiant rest, your faith will raise the song of conquest, and in its retrospect of the life which has ended, and its forward stance upon the life to come, take up the poetic inspiration of the Hebrew king, "Surely goodness and mercy have followed me all the days Of my life, and I will dwell in the house of the Lord forever."

—STOPFORD A. BROOKE

March 31

For you will have a covenant with the stones of the field, and the wild animals will be at peace with you.

JOB 6:23

All your strength is in your union.
All your danger is in discord;
Therefore be at peace henceforward,
And as brothers live together.
HENRY WADSWORTH LONGFELLOW

Our fallibility and the shortness of our knowledge should make us peaceable and gentle. Because I may be mistaken, I must not be dogmatical and confident, peremptory and imperious. I will not break the certain laws of charity for a doubtful doctrine of uncertain truth. Religion begins in knowledge, proceeds in practice, and ends in happiness.

—BENJAMIN WHICHCOTE

April

April 1

I have loved you with an everlasting love.
JEREMIAH 31:3

> That Love is all there is,
> Is all we know of Love;
> It is enough, the freight should be
> Proportioned to the groove.
> EMILY DICKINSON

To know that Love alone was the beginning of nature and creature, that nothing but Love encompasses the whole universe of things, that the governing Hand that overrules all, the watchful Eye that sees through all, is nothing but omnipotent and omniscient Love, using an infinity of wisdom, to save every misguided creature from the miserable works of his own hands, and make happiness and glory the perpetual inheritance of all the creation, is a reflection that must be quite ravishing to every intelligent creature that is sensible of it.

—WILLIAM LAW

April 2

*Don't you know that you yourselves are God's temple
and that God's Spirit lives in you?*
1 CORINTHIANS 3:16

> Oh thou who camest from above,
> The pure celestial fire to impart,
> Kindle a flame of sacred love
> On the mean altar of my heart.

There let it for thy glory burn
With inextinguishable blaze,
And trembling to its source return
In humble prayer, and fervent praise.
CHARLES WESLEY

Our deepest fear is not that we are inadequate. Our deepest fear is that we are powerful beyond measure. It is our light, not our darkness, that frightens us most. We ask ourselves, 'Who am I to be brilliant, gorgeous, talented, and famous?' Actually, who are you not to be? You are a child of God. Your playing small does not serve the world. There is nothing enlightened about shrinking so that people won't feel insecure around you. We were born to make manifest the glory of God that is within us. It's not just in some of us; it's in all of us. And when we let our own light shine, we unconsciously give other people permission to do the same. As we are liberated from our own fear, our presence automatically liberates others.

—MARIANNE WILLIAMSON

April 3

But as for you, the Lord your God has not permitted you to do so.
DEUTERONOMY 18:20

What an amazing, what a blessed disproportion between the evil we do, and the evil we are capable of doing, and seem sometimes on the very verge of doing! If my soul has grown tares, when it was full of the seeds of nightshade, how happy ought I to be! And that the tares have not wholly strangled the wheat, what a wonder it is! We ought to thank God daily for the sins we have not committed.

—F. W. FABER

You are surprised at your imperfections—why? I should infer from that, that your self-knowledge is small. Surely, you might rather be astonished that you do not fall into more frequent and more grievous faults, and thank God for His upholding grace.

—JEAN NICOLAS GROU

April 4

How many are your works, O Lord! In wisdom you made them all; the earth is full of your creatures. There is the sea, vast and spacious, teeming with creatures beyond number—living things both large and small.

PSALMS 104:24-25

All things bright and beautiful,
All creatures great and small,
All things wise and wonderful,
The Lord God made them all.

CECIL F. ALEXANDER

What inexpressible joy for me, to look up through the apple blossom and the fluttering leaves, and to see God's love there; to listen to the thrush that has built his nest among them, and to feel God's love, who cares for the birds, in every note that swells his little throat; to look beyond to the bright blue depths of the sky, and feel they are a canopy of blessing—the roof of the house of my Father; that if clouds pass over it, it is the unchangeable light they veil; that, even when the day itself passes, I shall see that the night itself only unveils new worlds of light; and to know that if I could unwrap fold after fold of God's universe, I should only unfold more

and more blessing, and see deeper and deeper into the love which is
at the heart of all.

—ELIZABETH CHARLES

April 5

---

*Yet I reserve seven thousand in Israel—all whose knees have not
bowed down to Baal and all whose mouths have not kissed him.*
1 KINGS 19:18

Every life is a profession of faith and exercises an inevitable and
silent propaganda. As far as lies in its power, it tends to transform
the universe and humanity into its own image. Thus we all have
a cure of souls. Every man is a center of perpetual radiation like
a luminous body; he is, as it were, a beacon which entices a ship
upon the rocks if it does not guide it into port. Every man is a
priest, even involuntarily; his conduct is an unspoken sermon,
which is for ever preaching to others—but there are priests of Baal,
of Moloch, and of all the false gods. Such is the high importance
of example. Thence comes the terrible responsibility which
weighs upon us all. An evil example is a spiritual poison: it is the
proclamation of a sacrilegious faith, of an impure God. Sin would
be an evil only for him who commits it, were it not a crime towards
the weak brethren, whom it corrupts. Therefore it has been said:
"It were better for a man not to have been born than to offend one
of these little ones."

—HENRI-FREDERIC AMIEL

April 6

We are hard pressed on every side,
but not crushed; perplexed,
but not in despair; persecuted, but not abandoned;
struck down, but not destroyed.
2 CORINTHIANS 4:8-9

Therefore do not lose heart . . .
2 CORINTHIANS 4:16

Discouraged in the work of life,
Disheartened by its load,
Shamed by its failures or its fears,
I sink beside the road;
But let me only think of Thee,
And then new heart springs up in me.
S. LONGFELLOW

Tenderness and kindness are not signs of weakness and despair,
but manifestations of strength and resolution.

—KHALIL GIBRAN

April 7

"I am willing. . . "
MATTHEW 8:3

. . . be transformed by the renewing of your mind.
Then you will be able to test and approve what
God's will is—his good, pleasing and perfect will.
ROMANS 12:2

Thou knowest what is best
And who but Thee, O God, hath power to know?
In Thy great will my trusting heart shall rest;
Beneath that will my humble head shall bow.

T. C. UPHAM

Let no riches make me ever forget myself, no poverty make me to forget thee: let no hope or fear, no pleasure or pain, no accident without, no weakness within, hinder or discompose my duty, or turn me from the ways of thy commandments . . .

—JEREMY TAYLOR

Suffer me never to think that I have knowledge enough to need no teaching, wisdom enough to need no correction, talents enough to need no grace, goodness enough to need no progress, humility enough to need no repentance, devotion enough to need no quickening, strength sufficient without thy Spirit; lest, standing still, I fall back for evermore.

—ERIC MILNER-WHITE

April 8

I am the good shepherd.
The good shepherd lays down his life for the sheep.
JOHN 10:11

The Lord is my shepherd, I shall not want.
PSALMS 23:1

The King of love my shepherd is,
Whose goodness faileth never;
I nothing lack if I am his,
And he is mine forever.
SIR HENRY WILLIAMS BAKER

God knows your value; He sees your potential. You may not understand everything you are going through right now. But hold your head up high, knowing that God is in control and he has a great plan and purpose for your life. Your dreams may not have turned out exactly as you'd hoped, but the bible says that God's ways are better and higher than our ways, even when everybody else rejects you, remember, God stands before you with His arms open wide. He always accepts you. He always confirms your value. God sees your two good moves! You are His prized possession. No matter what you go through in life, no matter how many disappointments you suffer, your value in God's eyes always remains the same. You will always be the apple of His eye. He will never give up on you, so don't give up on yourself.

—JOEL OSTEEN

April 9

---

*When tempted, no one should say,
"God is tempting me." For God cannot be tempted by evil,
nor does he tempt anyone; but each one is tempted when,
by his own evil desire, he is dragged away and enticed.*
JAMES 1:13-14

Christian life means a walking; it goes by steps. There is a straight fence run for us between right and wrong. There is no sitting on that fence. No; only walking, one side or other. You can hardly look across without stepping through.

—R.W. BARBOUR

You are doomed to make choices. This is life's greatest paradox.

—WAYNE DYER

April 10

---

*What good is it, my brothers,
if a man claims to have faith but has no deeds?*
JAMES 2:14

*Who is wise and understanding among you? Let him show it by his
good life, by deeds done in the humility that comes from wisdom.*
JAMES 3:13

Both the spiritual and the bodily powers of a man increase and become perfected and strengthened by their exercise. By exercising your hand in writing, sewing, or knitting you will accustom it to such work; by frequently exercising yourself in composition you will learn to write easily and well; by exercising yourself in doing good works or in conquering your passions and temptations, you will in time learn to do good works easily and with delight: and with the help of God's all-active grace you will easily learn to conquer your passions. But if you cease writing, sewing, knitting, or if you only do so seldom, you will write, sew, and knit badly. If you do not exercise yourself in composition, or do so very seldom, if you live in the material cares of life only, it will probably become difficult for you to connect a few words together, especially upon spiritual subjects; the work set you will seem to you like an Egyptian labor. If you cease praying, or pray seldom, prayer will be oppressive to you. If you do not fight against your passions, or only do so seldom and feebly, you will find it very difficult to fight against them; they will give you no rest, and your life will be poisoned by them, if you do not learn how to conquer these evil inward enemies that settle in your heart. Therefore labor and activity are indispensable for all. Life without activity is not life, but something monstrous—a sort of phantom of life. This is why it is the duty of every man to fight continually and persistently against the slothfulness of the flesh. God preserve every Christian from indulging it! "They that are Christ's have crucified the flesh with the affections and lusts." "Unto every one that hath shall be given, and he shall have abundance; but from him that hath not shall be taken away even that which he hath."

—FATHER JOHN SERGIEFF

April 11

. . . make every effort to be found spotless,
blameless and at peace with him.
2 PETER 3:14

Thy Sinless mind in us reveal,
Thy spirit's plenitude impart!
Till all my spotless life shall tell
The abundance of a loving heart.
C. WESLEY

I believe life is constantly testing us for our level of commitment, and life's greatest rewards are reserved for those who demonstrate a never-ending commitment to act until they achieve. This level of resolve can move mountains, but it must be constant and consistent. As simplistic as this may sound, it is still the common denominator separating those who live their dreams from those who live in regret.

—ANTHONY ROBBINS

Even the smallest discontent of conscience may render turbid the whole temper of the mind; but only produce the effort that restores its peace, and over the whole atmosphere a breath of unexpected purity is spread; doubt and irritability pass as clouds away; the withered sympathies of earth and home open their leaves and live; and through the clearest blue the deep is seen of the heaven where God resides.

—JAMES MARTINEAU

April 12

Aim for perfection, listen to my appeal,
be of one mind, live in peace.
2 CORINTHIANS 13:11

Whoever loves God must also love his brother.
1 JOHN 4:21

It requires far more of the constraining love of Christ to love our cousins and neighbors as members of the heavenly family, than to feel the heart warm to our suffering brethren in Tuscany or Madeira. To love the whole Church is one thing; to love—that is, to delight in the graces and veil the defects—of the person who misunderstood me and opposed my plans yesterday, whose peculiar infirmities grate on my most sensitive feelings, or whose natural faults are precisely those from which my natural character most revolts, is quite another.

—ELIZABETH CHARLES

When you judge another, you do not define them, you define yourself.

—WAYNE DYER

April 13

No, in all these things we are more than conquerors
through him who loved us.
ROMANS 8:37

I must not fear.
Fear is the mind-killer.
Fear is the little-death that brings total obliteration.
I will face my fear.
I will permit it to pass over me and through me.
And when it has gone past I will turn the inner eye to see its path.
Where the fear has gone there will be nothing.
Only I will remain.
FRANK HERBERT

If you are distressed by anything external, the pain is not due to the thing itself, but to your estimate of it; and this you have the power to revoke at any moment.

—MARCUS AURELIUS

April 14

. . . having nothing, and yet possessing everything.
2 CORINTHIANS 6:10

Blessed is the man who finds wisdom,
the man who gains
understanding, for she is more profitable than silver and
yields better returns than gold.
PROVERBS 3:13-14

By three methods we may learn wisdom: First, by reflection, which is noblest; Second, by imitation, which is easiest; and third by experience, which is the bitterest.

—CONFUCIUS

April 15

And we know that in all things God works
for the good of those who love him, who have been
called according to his purpose.
ROMANS 8:28

Do all the good you can,
By all the means you can,
In all the ways you can,
In all the places you can,
At all the times you can,
To all the people you can,
As long as ever you can.
JOHN WESLEY

People are often unreasonable and self-centered.
Forgive them anyway.
If you are kind, people may accuse you of ulterior motives.
Be kind anyway.
If you are honest, people may cheat you.
Be honest anyway.
If you find happiness, people may be jealous.
Be happy anyway.
The good you do today may be forgotten tomorrow.
Do good anyway.
Give the world the best you have and it may never be enough.
Give your best anyway.
For you see, in the end, it is between you and God. I
t was never between you and them anyway.
MOTHER TERESA

April 16

The one who calls you is faithful and he will do it.
1 THESSALONIANS 5:24

> *Be still, my soul!—the Lord is on thy side*
> *Bear patiently the cross of grief and pain*
> *Leave to thy God to order and provide,—*
> *In every change He faithful will remain.*
> HYMNS FROM THE LAND OF LUTHER

I have faith that God will show you the answer. But you have to understand that sometimes it takes a while to be able to recognize what God wants you to do. That's how it often is. God's voice is usually nothing more than a whisper, and you have to listen very carefully to hear it. But other times, in those rarest of moments, the answer is obvious and rings as loud as a church bell.

—NICHOLAS SPARKS

April 17

You will keep in perfect peace him whose mind is steadfast, because he trusts in you.
ISAIAH 26:3

. . . and trust in the Lord.
PSALMS 4:5

Just to let thy Father do
What He will;
just to know that He is true,
And be still;
Just to trust Him, this is all!
Then the day will surely be
Peaceful, whatsoe'er befall,
Bright and blessed, calm and free.

F. R. HAVERGAL

Things work out, it isn't as bad as you sometimes think it is. It all works out, don't worry. I say that to myself every morning. It will all work out. If you do your best, it will all work out. Put your trust in God, and move forward with faith and confidence in the future. The Lord will not forsake us. If we will put our trust in him, if we will pray to him, if we will live worthy of his blessings, he will hear our prayers.

—GORDON B. HINKLEY

April 18

I praise you because I am fearfully and wonderfully made;
your works are wonderful . . .

PSALMS 139:14

What asks our Father of His children save
Justice and mercy and humility,
A reasonable service of good deeds,
Pure living, tenderness to human needs,
Reverence, and trust, and prayer for light to see
The Master's footprints in our daily ways?
No knotted scourge, nor sacrificial knife,
But the calm beauty of an ordered life
Whose every breathing is unworded praise.

J.G. WHITTIER

As long as rivers shall run down to the sea, or shadows touch the mountain slopes, or stars graze in the vault of heaven, so long shall your honor, your name, your praises endure.

—VIRGIL

April 19

The gracious hand of our God
is on everyone who looks to him . . .

EZRA 8:22

My times are in your hands; deliver me from my enemies . . .

PSALMS 31:15

Today, beneath Thy chastening eye,
I crave alone for peace and rest
Submissive in Thy hand to lie,
And feel that it is best.

J. G. WHITTIER

There are some things you learn best in calm, and some in storm.

—WILLA CATHER

Just as treasures are uncovered from the earth, so virtue appears from good deeds, and wisdom appears from a pure and peaceful mind. To walk safely through the maze of human life, one needs the light of wisdom and the guidance of virtue.

—BUDDHA

April 20

. . . we also rejoice in our sufferings, because we know that suffering produces perseverance; perseverance, character; and character, hope.

ROMANS 5:3-4

The path of sorrow, and that path alone,
Leads to the land where sorrow is unknown.
No traveller e'er reached that bless'd abode,
Who found not thorns and briars in his road.

ANONYMOUS

Times of great calamity and confusion have ever been productive of the greatest minds. The purest ore is produced from the hottest furnace, and the brightest thunderbolt is elicited from the darkest storm.

—CHARLES CALEB COLTON

If we consider how much men can suffer if they list, and how much they do suffer for greater and little causes, and that no causes are greater than the proper causes of patience in sickness (that is, necessity and religion) we cannot, without huge shame to our nature, to our persons, and to our manners, complain of this tax and impost of nature. . . .

Sickness is the more tolerable, because it cures very many evils, and takes away the sense of all the cross fortunes, which amaze the spirits of some men, and transport them certainly beyond all the limits of patience. Here all losses and disgraces, domestic cares and public evils, the apprehensions of pity and a sociable calamity, the fears of want and the troubles of ambition, lie down and rest upon the sick man's pillow. . . .

—JEREMY TAYLOR

April 21

I love you, O Lord, my strength.
PSALMS 18:1

Blest be Thy love, dear Lord,
That taught us this sweet way,
Only to love Thee for Thyself,
And for that love obey.
J. AUSTIN

This life is yours. Take the power to choose what you want to do and do it well. Take the power to love what you want in life and love it honestly. Take the power to walk in the forest and be a part of nature. Take the power to control your own life. No one else can do it for you. Take the power to make your life happy.

—SUSAN POLIS SCHUTZ

April 22

The Lord has done great things for us, and we are filled with joy.
PSALMS 126:3

Come and share your master's happiness!
MATTHEW 25:23

As for that which is beyond your strength, be absolutely certain that our Lord loves you, devotedly and individually: loves you just as you are. How often that conviction is lacking even in those souls who are most devoted to God! They make repeated efforts to love Him, they experience the joy of loving, and yet how little they know, how little they realize, that God loves them incomparably more than they will ever know how to love Him. Think only of this and say to yourself, "I am loved by God more than I can either conceive or understand." Let this fill all your soul and all your prayers and never leave you. You will soon see that this is the way to find God. It contains the whole of St. John's teaching: "As for us, we have believed in the love which God has for us. . . ." Accustom yourself to the wonderful thought that God loves you with a tenderness, a generosity, and an intimacy which surpasses all your dreams. Give yourself up with joy to a loving confidence in God and have courage to believe firmly that God's action towards you is a masterpiece of partiality and love. Rest tranquilly in this abiding conviction.

—HENRI DE TOURVILLE

April 23

One man pretends to be rich, yet has nothing;
another pretends to be poor, yet has great wealth.
PROVERBS 13:7

. . . I asked for riches that I might be happy;
I was given poverty that I might be wise.
I asked for power that I might have the praise of men;
I was given weakness that I might feel the need of God
I asked for all things that I might enjoy life;
I was given life that I might enjoy all things.
. . . Almost despite myself my unspoken prayers were answered;
I am, among all men, most richly blessed.
PRAYER OF AN UNKNOWN CONFEDERATE SOLDIER

My friends, do you remember that old Scythian custom, when the head of a house died? How he was dressed in his finest dress, and set in his chariot, and carried about to his friends' houses; and each of them placed him at his table's head, and all feasted in his presence? Suppose it were offered to you in plain words, as it is offered to you in dire facts, that you should gain this Scythian honor, gradually, while you yet thought yourself alive. Suppose the offer were this: You shall die slowly; your blood shall daily grow cold, your flesh petrify, your heart beat at last only as a rusted group of iron valves. Your life shall fade from you, and sink through the earth into the ice of Caina; but, day by day, your body shall be dressed more gaily, and set in higher chariots, and have more orders on its breast—crowns on its head, if you will. Men shall bow before it, stare and shout round it, crowd after it up and down the streets; build palaces for it, feast with it at their tables' heads all the night long; your soul shall stay enough within it to know what they do, and feel the weight of the golden dress on its shoulders, and the furrow of the crown-edge on the skull—no more. Would you take the offer, verbally made by the death angel? Would the meanest among us take it, think you? Yet practically and verily we grasp at it, every one of us, in a measure; many of us grasp at it in its fullness of horror. Every man accepts it who desires to advance in life without knowing what life is; who means only that he is to get more horses, and more footmen, and more fortune, and more public honor, and—not more personal soul. He only is advancing in life whose heart is getting softer, whose blood warmer, whose brain quicker, whose spirit is entering into living peace.

—JOHN RUSKIN

April 24

Carry each other's burdens,
and in this way you will fulfill the law of Christ.
GALATIANS 6:2

I tell you the truth, whatever you did for one of the least of these
brothers of mine, you did for me.
MATTHEW 25:40

Is thy cruse of comfort wasting?
Rise and share it with another,
And through all the years of famine,
It shall serve thee and thy brother.
Is thy burden hard and heavy?
Do thy steps drag heavily?
Help to bear thy brother's burden
God will bear both it and thee.

ELIZABETH CHARLES

This is the true joy in life—being used for a purpose recognized
by yourself as a mighty one; being thoroughly worn out before you
are thrown on the scrap heap; being a force of nature instead of a
feverish selfish little clod of ailments and grievances complaining
that the world will not devote itself to making you happy.

—GEORGE BERNARD SHAW

April 25

Train a child in the way he should go,
and when he is old he will not turn from it.

PROVERBS 22:6

When I was a child,
I talked like a child,
I thought like a child,
I reasoned like a child.
When I became a man,
I put childish ways behind me.

1 CORINTHIANS 13:11

"What does God do all day?" once asked a little boy. One could wish that more grown-up people would ask so very real a question. Unfortunately most of us are not even boys in religious intelligence, but only very unthinking babes. It no more occurs to us that God is engaged in any particular work in the world than it occurs to a little child that its father does anything except be its father. Its father may be a cabinet minister absorbed in the nation's work or an inventor deep in schemes for the world's good; but to this master-egoist he is father and nothing more. Childhood, whether in the physical or in the moral world, is the great self-centered period of life; and a personal God who satisfies personal ends is all that for a long time many a Christian understands.

But as clearly as there comes to the growing child a knowledge of his father's part in the world, and a sense of what real life means, there must come to every Christian, whose growth is true, some richer sense of the meaning of Christianity and a larger view of Christ's purpose for mankind.

—HENRY DRUMMOND

For as children tremble and fear everything in the blind darkness, so we in the light sometimes fear what is no more to be feared than the things children in the dark hold in terror and imagine will come true.

—LUCRETIUS

April 26

With the Lord a day is like a thousand years, and a thousand years are like a day. The Lord is not slow in keeping his promise . . .
1 PETER 3:8-9

Lord! who Thy thousand years dost wait
To work the thousandth part
Of Thy vast plan, for us create
With zeal a patient heart.
J. H. NEWMAN

Even a happy life cannot be without a measure of darkness, and the word happy would lose its meaning if it were not balanced by sadness. It is far better take things as they come along with patience and equanimity.

—CARL JUNG

The strongest of all warriors are these two—Time and Patience.

—LEO TOLSTOY

April 27

Therefore each of you must put off falsehood and speak truthfully to his neighbor, for we are all members of one body.
EPHESIANS 4:25

Appear I always what I am?
And am I what I am pretending?
Know I what way my course is bending?
And sound my word and thought the same?
ANONYMOUS

Wisdom without honesty is mere craft and cozenage. And therefore the reputation of honesty must first be gotten; which cannot be but by living well. A good life is a main argument.

Truth is man's proper good and the only immortal thing was given to our mortality to use. No good Christian or ethnic, if he be honest, can miss it; no statesman or patriot should. For without truth all the actions of mankind are craft, malice, or what you will rather than wisdom. Homer says he hates him worse than hell mouth that utters one thing with his tongue and keeps another in his breast. Which high expression was grounded on divine reason; for a lying mouth is a stinking pit, and murders with the contagion it venteth. Beside, nothing is lasting that is feigned; it will have another face than it had, ere long. As Euripides said, "No lie ever grows old."

—BEN JONSON

I must speak the truth, and nothing but the truth.
. . . An honest man's word is as good as his bond.

—MIGUEL DE CERVANTES

April 28

I am a man of peace.
PSALMS 120:6

Drop thy still dews of quietness,
Till all our strivings cease;
Take from our souls the strain and stress,
And let our ordered lives confess
The beauty of thy peace.
J. G. WHITTIER

Every morning compose your soul for a tranquil day, and all through it be careful often to recall your resolution, and bring yourself back to it, so to say. If something discomposes you, do not be upset, or troubled; but having discovered the fact, humble yourself gently before God, and try to bring your mind into a quiet attitude. Say to yourself, "Well, I have made a false step; now I must go more carefully and watchfully." Do this each time, however frequently you fall. When you are at peace use it profitably, making constant acts of meekness, and seeking to be calm even in the most trifling things. Above all, do not be discouraged; be patient; wait; strive to attain a calm, gentle spirit.

—ST. FRANCIS DE SALES

April 29

Father, I have sinned against heaven and against you.
I am no longer worthy to be called your son.
LUKE 15:21

Look not mournfully into the past, it comes not back again.
Wisely improve the present, it is thine. Go forth to meet the
shadowy future without fear and with a manly heart.

HENRY WADSWORTH LONGFELLOW

We've all heard about people who've exploded beyond the limitations of their conditions to become examples of the unlimited power of the human spirit. You and I can make our lives one of these legendary inspirations, as well, simply by having courage and the awareness that we can control whatever happens in our lives. Although we cannot always control the events in our lives, we can always control our response to them, and the actions we take as a result. If there's anything you're not happy about—in your relationships, in your health, in your career--make a decision right now about how you're going to change it immediately.

—ANTHONY ROBBINS

April 30

Tell the Israelites to move on.
EXODUS 14:15

Be trustful, be steadfast, whatever betide thee,
Only one thing do thou ask of the Lord,
Grace to go forward wherever He guide thee,
Simply believing the truth of His word.
ANONYMOUS

The hearts and minds of the Apostles are filled with the thought and the love of Him who had redeemed them and in whom they had found their true life, and with the work which they were to do in His service, for His glory, for the spreading of His Kingdom. This too was one of the greatest and most blessed among the truths which Luther was especially ordained to reproclaim—that we are not to spend our days in watching our own vices, in gazing at our own sins, in stirring and raking up all the mud of our past lives; but to lift our thoughts from our own corrupt nature to Him who put on that nature in order to deliver it from corruption, and to fix our contemplations and our affections on Him who came to clothe us in His perfect righteousness, and through whom and in whom, if we are united to Him by a living faith, we too become righteous.

Thus, like the Apostle, we are to forget that which is behind, and to keep our eyes bent on the prize of our high calling, to which we are to press onward, and which we may attain, in Christ Jesus.

—AUGUSTUS AND J. C. HARE

May

May 1

All the days of the oppressed are wretched,
but the cheerful heart has a continual feast.
PROVERBS 15:15

Thrice blest will all our blessings be,
When we can look through them to Thee;
When each glad heart its tribute pays
Of love and gratitude and praise.
M. J. COTTERILL

Be of good cheer. Do not think of today's failures, but of the success that may come tomorrow. You have set yourselves a difficult task, but you will succeed if you persevere; and you will find a joy in overcoming obstacles. Remember, no effort that we make to attain something beautiful is ever lost.

—HELEN KELLER

May 2

Make it your ambition to lead a quiet life . . .
1 THESSALONIANS 4:11

. . . that we may live peaceful and quiet lives
in all godliness and holiness.
1 TIMOTHY 2:2

Give me my scallop shell of quiet,
My staff of faith to walk upon,
My scrip of joy, immortal diet,
My bottle of salvation,
my gown of glory, hope's true gage
And thus I'll take my pilgrimage.
SIR WALTER RALEIGH

All beneficent and creative power gathers itself together in
silence, ere it issues out in might. Force itself indeed is naturally
silent and only makes itself heard, if at all, when it strikes upon
obstructions to bear them away as it returns to equilibrium again.
The very hurricane that roars over land and ocean flits noiselessly
through spaces where nothing meets it. The blessed sunshine says
nothing as it warms the vernal earth, tempts out the tender grass,
and decks the field and forest in their glory. Silence came before
creation, and the heavens were spread without a word. Christ was
born at dead of night; and though there has been no power like
His, "He did not strive nor cry, neither was His voice heard in the
streets."

Nowhere can you find any beautiful work, any noble design,
any durable endeavour, that was not matured in long and patient
silence ere it spake out in its accomplishment. There it is that
we accumulate the inward power which we distribute and spend
in action, put the smallest duty before us in dignified and holy
aspects, and reduce the severest hardships beneath the foot of our
self-denial. There it is that the soul, enlarging all its dimensions at
once, acquires a greater and more vigorous being, and gathers up
its collective forces to bear down upon the piecemeal difficulties of
life and scatter them to dust. There alone can we enter into that
spirit of self-abandonment by which we take up the cross of duty,
however heavy, with feet however worn and bleeding they may
be. And thither shall we return again, only into higher peace and

more triumphant power, when the labour is over and the victory won, and we are called by death into God's loftiest watchtower of contemplation.

—JAMES MARTINEAU

May 3

The Lord is good, a refuge in times of trouble.
He cares for those who trust in him . . .
NAHUM 1:7

Never to suffer would never to have been blessed.
EDGAR ALLEN POE

The most beautiful people we have known are those who have known defeat, known suffering, known struggle, known loss, and have found their way out of the depths. These persons have an appreciation, a sensitivity, and an understanding of life that fills them with compassion, gentleness, and a deep loving concern. Beautiful people do not just happen.

—ELIZABETH KUBLER-ROSS

Fight the good fight of the faith.
1 TIMOTHY 6:12

You armed me with strength for battle,
you made my adversaries bow at my feet.
PSALMS 18:39

Go face the fire at sea, or the cholera in your friend's house, or the burglar in your own, or what danger lies in the way of duty, knowing you are guarded by the cherubim of Destiny.

—RALPH WALDO EMERSON

You may encounter many defeats, but you must not be defeated. In fact, it may be necessary to encounter the defeats, so you can know who you are, what you can rise from, how you can still come out of it.

—MAYA ANGELOU

You are all sons of the light and sons of the day.
1 THESSALONIANS 5:5

Teach me thy love to know;
That this new light, which now I see,
May both the work and workman show:
Then by a sunne-beam I will climbe to thee.

GEORGE HERBERT

To walk in the light means that we confess our sins without reserve. Sometimes we do not really confess our sins when we think we are doing so: we rather admit our sins than confess them, and we seek in all possible ways to explain, to extenuate, and to excuse them. . . . We think of the evil nature we have inherited, of the bias in our constitution to this or that attractive vice, of the defects of our education, of the violence of temptation, of the compulsion of circumstances; we do not deny what we have done—we cannot—but we mitigate it by every possible plea. This is not walking in the light. In all such self-excusing there is a large element of voluntary self-deception which keeps the life in the dark. To walk in the light requires us to accept our responsibilities without reserve, to own our sin that we may be able to disown it, and not to own it with such qualifications and reserves as amount to saying in the long run, It was indeed I who did it, but after all it is not I who should bear the blame. A man who makes it his business not to confess his sin, but to understand it and explain it, no matter how philosophical he may seem, is walking in darkness, and the truth is not in him. . . . Finally, to walk in the light means that when we confess our sins to God we do not keep a secret hold of them in our hearts. Where there is something hidden in the heart, hidden from God and from man, the darkness is as deep and dreadful as it can be. The desire to keep such a secret hold of sin is itself a sin to be confessed, to be declared in its exceeding sinfulness, to be unreservedly renounced . . . . The man who has a guilty secret in his life is a lonely man. There can be no cordial Christian overflow from his heart to the hearts of others, nor from theirs to his. And he is a man doomed to bear in his loneliness the uneffaced stain of his sin. The cleansing virtue of the atonement cannot reach him where he dwells by himself in the dark.

—JAMES DENNEY

May 6

Be devoted to one another in brotherly love.
Honor one another above yourselves.
ROMANS 12:10

Swiftly arose and spread around me the peace and
knowledge that pass all the argument of the earth,
And I know that the hand of God is the promise of my own,
And I know that the spirit of God is the brother of my own,
And that all the men ever born are also brothers . . .

WALT WHITMAN

You have not fulfilled every duty, unless you have fulfilled that of being pleasant.

—CHARLES BUXTON

The Bible says no man can take your joy. That means no person can make you live with a negative attitude. No circumstance, no adversity can force you to live in despair. As Eleanor Roosevelt, wife of wheelchair-bound President Franklin D. Roosevelt, often said, "No one can make you feel inferior without your consent."

—JOEL OSTEEN

May 7

. . . rejoice that your names are written in heaven.
LUKE 10:20

He determines the number of the stars and calls them each by name.
PSALMS 147:4

O Hidden Life, vibrant in every atom,
O Hidden Light, shining in every creature,
O Hidden Love, embracing all in Oneness,
May each who feels himself as one with Thee
Know he is therefore one with every other.
ANNIE BESANT

Blessed be you, harsh matter, barren soil, stubborn rock: you who yield only to violence, you who force us to work if we would eat. Blessed be you, perilous matter, violent sea, untamable passion: you who unless we fetter you will devour us. Blessed be you, mighty matter, irresistible march of evolution, reality ever newborn; you who, by constantly shattering our mental categories, force us to go ever further and further in our pursuit of the truth. Blessed be you, universal matter, unmeasurable time, boundless ether, triple abyss of stars and atoms and generations: you who by overflowing and dissolving our narrow standards of measurement reveal to us the dimensions of God . . .

—TEILHARD DE CHARDIN, SJ

May 8

He . . . must work,
doing something useful with his own hands . . .
EPHESIANS 4:28

Why have you been standing here
all day long doing nothing?
MATTHEW 20:6

Let us, then, be up and doing,
With a heart for any fate;
Still achieving, still pursuing,
Learn to labor and to wait.
HENRY WADSWORTH LONGFELLOW

The day returns and brings us the petty round of irritation concerns and duties. Help us to play the man, help us to perform them with laughter and kind faces. Let cheerfulness abound with industry. Give us to go blithely on our business all this day, bring us to our resting beds weary and content and undishonoured, and grant us in the end the gift of sleep.

—ROBERT LOUIS STEVENSON

Without ambition one starts nothing. Without work one finishes nothing. The prize will not be sent to you. You have to win it.

—RALPH WALDO EMERSON

May 9

---

*My son, do not despise the Lord's discipline and
do not resent his rebuke,
because the Lord disciplines those he loves,
as a father the son he delights in.*
PROVERBS 3:11-12

We are ready to praise when all shines fair; but when life is
overcast, when all things seem to be against us, when we are in
fear for some cherished happiness, or in the depths of sorrow, or in
the solitude of a life which has no visible support, or in a season
of sickness, and with the shadow of death approaching—then to
praise God; then to say, "This fear, loneliness, affliction, pain, and
trembling awe are as sure token of love, as life, health, joy, and the
gifts of home:" "The Lord gave, and the Lord hath taken away"; on
either side it is He, and all is love alike; "blessed be the name of the
Lord"—this is the true sacrifice of praise. What can come amiss to
a soul which is so in accord with God? What can make so much as
one jarring tone in all its harmony? In all the changes of this fitful
life, it ever dwells in praise.

—H. E. MANNING

May 10

When I am afraid, I will trust in you.
PSALMS 56:3

Cowards die many times before their deaths;
The valiant never taste of death but once.
Of all the wonders that I yet have heard,
It seems to me most strange that men should fear;
Seeing that death, a necessary end,
Will come when it will come.
WILLIAM SHAKESPEARE

The best remedy for those who are afraid, lonely or unhappy is
to go outside, somewhere where they can be quite alone with the
heavens, nature and God. Because only then does one feel that all
is as it should be and that God wishes to see people happy, amidst
the simple beauty of nature. As longs as this exists, and it certainly
always will, I know that then there will always be comfort for every
sorrow, whatever the circumstances may be. And I firmly believe
that nature brings solace in all troubles.

—ANNE FRANK

May 11

Whoever wants to become great among
you must be your servant . . .
MATTHEW 20:26

Make us worthy, Lord,
To serve our fellow-men
Throughout the world who live and die
In poverty and hunger.

Give them, through our hands
this day their daily bread,
And by our understanding love,
Give peace and joy.

MOTHER TERESA

So long as we love we serve; so long as we are loved by others, I would almost say that we are indispensable; and no man is useless while he has a friend.

—ROBERT LOUIS STEVENSON

If we do not lay out ourselves in the service of mankind, whom should we serve?

—ABIGAIL ADAMS

May 12

God is our refuge and strength,
an ever-present help in trouble.
Therefore we will not fear, though the earth give way
and the mountains fall into the heart of the sea,
though its waters roar and foam
and the mountains quake with their surging.

PSALMS 46:1-3

Fix'd on this ground will I remain,
Though my heart fail, and flesh decay;
This anchor shall my soul sustain,
When earth's foundations melt away:
Mercy's full power I then shall prove,
Lov'd with an everlasting love.

ANONYMOUS

Give us grace and strength to forbear and to persevere. . . . Give
us courage and gaiety and the quiet mind, spare to us our friends,
soften to us our enemies.

—ROBERT LOUIS STEVENSON

Tell your heart that the fear of suffering is worse than the suffering
itself. And that no heart has ever suffered when it goes in search
of its dreams, because every second of the search is a second's
encounter with God and with eternity.

—PAULO COELHO

Blessed is the man whom God corrects,
So do not despise the discipline of the Almighty.
For he wounds, but he also binds up;
he injures, but his hands also heal.
JOB 5:17-18

. . . Yet I argue not
Against Heaven's hand or will, nor bate a jot
of heart or hope; but still bear up and steer
Right onward.
JOHN MILTON

The practice of forgiveness is our most important contribution to the healing of the world.

—MARRIANNE WILLIAMSON

The miracles of the church seem to me to rest not so much upon faces or voices or healing power coming suddenly near to us from afar off, but upon our perceptions being made finer, so that for a moment our eyes can see and our ears can hear what is there about us always.

—WILLA CATHER

May 14

Put on therefore . . . kindness,
humbleness of mind, meekness, long-suffering.
COLOSSIANS 3:12

Meekness, humility, and love,
Did through thy conduct shine;
Oh may my whole deportment prove
A copy, Lord, of thine.
ANONYMOUS

If you are humble nothing will touch you, neither praise nor disgrace, because you know what you are.

—MOTHER TERESA

A mature person is one who does not think only in absolutes, who is able to be objective even when deeply stirred emotionally, who has learned that there is both good and bad in all people and in all things, and who walks humbly and deals charitably with the circumstances of life, knowing that in this world no one is all knowing and therefore all of us need both love and charity.

—ELEANOR ROOSEVELT

May 15

*Come to me, all you who are weary and burdened,
and I will give you rest. Take my yoke upon you and learn from me,
for I am gentle and humble in heart, and you will find rest for your
souls. For my yoke is easy and my burden is light.*
MATTHEW 11:28-30

There are two deep principles in Nature in apparent
contradiction—one, the aspiration after perfection; the other, the
longing after repose. In the harmony of these lies the rest of the
soul of man. There have been times when we have experienced
this. Then the winds have been hushed, and the throb and tumult
of the passions have been blotted out of our bosoms. That was a
moment when we were in harmony with all around, reconciled to
ourselves and to our God; when we sympathized with all that was
pure, and that was beautiful, all that was lovely.

—F. W. ROBERTSON

May 16

*Finally, be strong in the Lord and in his mighty power. . . .
Stand firm then, with the belt of truth buckled around your waist,
with the breastplate of righteousness in place, and with your feet with
the readiness that comes from the gospel of peace.*
EPHESIANS 6:10, 14-15

We know that in the moral, as in the physical order, nature abhors a vacancy. Consciously or unconsciously, as the years go by, all men more and more submit their lives to some allegiance; with whatever uncertainty and changefulness, some one motive, or group of motives, grows stronger and stronger in them; they tend, at least, to bring every thought into captivity to some one obedience. For better or for worse, things which seemed difficult or impossible a few years ago will come almost naturally to a man a few years hence; he will have got accustomed to take a certain course, to obey certain impulses or principles wherever they appear. We may indeed distinguish three states in which a man may be. He may be yielding his heart more and more to the love of self, in whatsoever way of pride, or avarice, or lust, or sloth. Or he may be yielding his heart more and more to the love of God, falteringly, it may be, with many struggles and failures, but still really getting to love God more, to move more readily and more loyally to do God's will wherever he sees it. Or, thirdly, he may be like the man of whom our Lord spoke. He may, by God's grace, have cast out an evil spirit from his heart; he may have broken away from the mastery ot some bad passion, some tyrannous hunger or hatred; and he may be hesitating, keeping his heart swept, clear and empty; his will may be poised, as it were, between the one love and the other. Ah! but that can only be for a very little while. That balance never lasts; one way or the other the will must incline; one service or the other must be chosen, and that soon.

—FRANCIS PAGET

May 17

Be devoted to one another in brotherly love.
Honor one another above yourselves.
ROMANS 12:10

. . . love your neighbor as yourself.
MATTHEW 19:19

Can I see another's woe,
And not be in sorrow too?
Can I see another's grief,
And not seek for kind relief?
WILLIAM BLAKE

There is an idea abroad among moral people that they should make
their neighbors good. One person I have to make good: Myself. But
my duty to my neighbor is much more nearly expressed by saying
that I have to make him happy if I may.

—ROBERT LOUIS STEVENSON

May 18

Whoever does not love does not know God, for God is love.
I JOHN 4. 8

And all must love the human form,
In heathen, turk, or jew;
Where Mercy, Love, & Pity dwell
There God is dwelling too.
WILLIAM BLAKE

Oh, how many times we can most of us remember when we would gladly have made any compromise with our consciences, would gladly have made the most costly sacrifices to God, if He would only have excused us from this duty of loving, of which our nature seemed utterly incapable. It is far easier to feel kindly, to act kindly, toward those with whom we are seldom brought into contact, whose tempers and prejudices do not rub against ours, whose interests do not clash with ours, than to keep up an habitual, steady, self-sacrificing love towards those whose weaknesses and faults are always forcing themselves upon us, and are stirring up our own. A man may pass good muster as a philanthropist who makes but a poor master to his servants, or father to his children.

—E. D. MAURICE

May 19

Be still, and know that I am God . . . .
PSALMS 46:10

Jesus, with thy word complying,
Firm our faith and hope shall be;
On thy faithfulness relying,
We will seek our rest in thee.
ANONYMOUS

He who believes in God is not careful for the morrow, but labors joyfully and with a great heart. "For He giveth His beloved, as in sleep." They must work and watch, yet never be careful or anxious, but commit all to Him, and live in serene tranquility; with a quiet heart, as one who sleeps safely and quietly.

—MARTIN LUTHER

There comes a time when the world gets quiet and the only thing left is your own heart. So you'd better learn the sound of it. Otherwise you'll never understand what it's saying.

—SARAH DESSEN

Silence never shows itself to so great an advantage as when it is made the reply to calumny and defamation, provided that we give no occasion for them. We might produce an example of it in the behavior of One in whom it appeared in all its majesty, and One whose silence, as well as His person, was altogether divine. When one considers this subject only in its sublimity, this great instance could not but occur to me; and since I only make use of it to show the highest example of it, I hope I do not offend in it. To forbear replying to an unjust reproach, and overlook it with a generous or, if possible, with an entire neglect of it, is one of the most heroic acts of a great mind; and (I must confess) when I reflect upon the behavior of some of the greatest men in antiquity, I do not so much admire them that they deserved the praise of the whole age they lived in, as because they contemned the envy and detraction of it.

—JOSEPH ADDISON

May 20

Consider the blameless, observe the upright;
there is a future for the man of peace.
PSALMS 37:37

Calm soul of all things! make it mine
To feel, amid the city's jar,
That there abides a peace of thine,
Man did not make, and cannot mar.
MATTHEW ARNOLD

Lord, make me an instrument of your peace.
Where there is hatred, let me sow love,
Where there is injury, pardon,
Where there is doubt, faith;
Where there is despair, hope;
Where there is darkness, light;
Where there is sadness, joy.
O divine Master, Grant that I may not so much seek
To be consoled, as to console,
To be understood, as to understand,
To be loved, as to love,
For it is in giving that we receive;
It is in pardoning that we are pardoned;
It is in dying that we are born to eternal life.

—ST. FRANCIS OF ASSISI

May 21

Let the beloved of the Lord rest secure in him;
for he shields him all day long,
and the one the Lord loves rests between his shoulders.
DEUTERONOMY 33:12

I love the people in my life, and I do for my friends whatever
they need me to do for them, again and again, as many times
as is necessary. For example, in your case you always forgot who
you are and how much you're loved. So what I do for you as your
friend is remind you who you are and tell you how much I love
you. And this isn't any kind of burden for me, because I love who
you are very much. Every time I remind you, I get to remember
with you, which is my pleasure.

— JAMES LECESNE

May 22

But the Lord said to Samuel, "Do not consider his appearance or his height, for I have rejected him. The Lord does not look at the things man looks at. Man looks at the outward appearance, but the Lord looks at the heart."
I SAMUEL 16:14

The heart should have fed upon the truth, as insects on a leaf, till it be tinged with the color, and show its food in every minutest fiber.
SAMUEL TAYLOR COLERIDGE

One man said, "I looked at my brother through the microscope of criticism, and I said, 'How coarse my brother is.' Then I looked at my brother through the telescope of scorn, and I said, 'How small my brother is.' Then I looked into the mirror of truth and I said, 'How like me my brother is."

—THOMAS S. MONSON

May 23

Resentment kills a fool, and envy slays the simple.
JOB 5:2

But as for me, my feet had almost slipped;
I had nearly lost my foothold.
For I envied the arrogant when
I saw the prosperity of the wicked.

PSALMS 73:2-3

Love thyself last: cherish those hearts that hate thee;
Corruption wins not more than honesty.
Still in thy right hand carry gentle peace,
To silence envious tongues: be just, and fear not.

WILLIAM SHAKESPEARE

Clemens has his head full of imaginary piety. He is often proposing
to himself what he would do if he had a great estate. He would
outdo all charitable men that are gone before him, he would
retire from the world, he would have no equipage, he would allow
himself only necessaries, that widows and orphans, the sick and
distressed, might find relief out of his estate. He tells you that
all other way of spending an estate is folly and madness. Now,
Clemens has at present a moderate estate, which he spends upon
himself in the same vanities and indulgences as other people do.
He might live upon one-third of his fortune and make the rest
the support of the poor; but he does nothing of all this that is in
his power, but pleases himself with what he would do if his power
was greater. Come to thy senses, Clemens. Do not talk what thou
wouldst do if thou wast an angel, but consider what thou canst do
as thou art a man. Make the best use of thy present state, do now
as thou thinkest thou wouldst do with a great estate, be sparing,
deny thyself, abstain from all vanities, that the poor may be better
maintained, and then thou art as charitable as thou canst be in any
estate. Remember the poor widow's mite.

—WILLIAM LAW

May 24

*Blessed is the man who perseveres under trial, because when
he has stood the test, he will receive the crown of life that
God has promised those who love him.*

JAMES 1:12

I cannot say,
Beneath the pressure of life's cares to-day,
I joy in these;
But I can say
That I had rather walk this rugged way,
If Him it please.

S. G. BROWNING

The proper and natural effect, and in the absence of all disturbing
and intercepting forces, the certain and inevitable accompaniment
of peace (or reconcilement) with God is our own inward peace, a
calm and quiet temper of mind. . . . The chameleon darkens in
the shade of him who bends over it to ascertain its colors. In like
manner, but with yet greater caution, ought we to think respecting
a tranquil habit of inward life, considered as a spiritual sense, as
the medial organ in and by which our peace with God, and the
lively working of His grace in our spirit, are perceived by us. This
peace which we have with God in Christ, is inviolable; but because
the sense and persuasion of it may be interrupted, the soul that
is truly at peace with God may for a time be disquieted in itself,
through weakness of faith, or the strength of temptation, or the
darkness of desertion, losing sight of that grace, that love and light
of God's countenance, on which its tranquillity and joy depend.

But when these eclipses are over, the soul is revived with new
consolation, as the face of the earth is renewed and made to smile
with the return of the sun in the spring; and this ought always to

uphold Christians in the saddest times, namely, that the grace and love of God towards them depend, not on their sense, nor upon anything in them, but is stiff in itself, incapable of the smallest alteration.

—SAMUEL TAYLOR COLERIDGE

May 25

Going a little farther, he fell with his face to the ground and prayed, "My Father, if it be possible, may this cup be taken from me. Yet not as I will, but as you will."
MATTHEW 26:39

Probably one of the greatest ways we show our trust in God is by living life one day at a time. We prove our confidence in Him by enjoying today and not letting the concern of tomorrow interfere.

—JOYCE MEYERS

May 26

Moses also said, "You will know that it was the Lord when he gives you meat to eat in the evening and all the bread you want in the morning, because he has heard your grumbling against him. Who are we? You are not grumbling against us, but against the Lord."
EXODUS 16:8

Without murmur, uncomplaining,
In His hand,
Leave whatever things thou canst not
Understand.

K. R. HAGENBACH

Even though this is hard, even though I don't understand it, even though it's not fair, I'll keep a good attitude and stay full of joy, knowing that this is not setting me back. It is setting me up for God to bring me through to the other side of this in an even better position.

—JOEL OSTEEN

May 27

Whoever can be trusted with very little can also be trusted with much, and whoever is dishonest with very little will also be dishonest with much.

LUKE 16:10

That best portion of a good man's life,
little, nameless, unremembered acts
Of kindness and of love.

WILLIAM WORDSWORTH

Real integrity is doing the right thing, knowing that nobody's going to know whether you did it or not.

—OPRAH WINFREY

May 28

The Lord is the everlasting God,
The creator of the ends of the earth.
He will not grow tired or weary,
and his understanding no one can fathom.
He gives strength to the weary and increases the power of the weak.
Even youths grow tired and weary,
and young men stumble and fall;
but those who hope in the Lord will renew their strength.
They will soar on wings like eagles,
they will run and not grow weary,
they will walk and not be faint.
ISAIAH 40:28-31

Give us grace and strength to forbear and to persevere . . .
Give us courage and gaiety and the quiet mind,
Spare to us our friends,
Soften to us our enemies.
ROBERT LOUIS STEVENSON

Do not think that love in order to be genuine has to be extraordinary. What we need is to love without getting tired. Be faithful in small things because it is in them that your strength lies.

—MOTHER TERESA

May 29

There is most joy in virtue when 'tis hardest won.
LUCAN

Burn from my brain and from my breast
Sloth, and the cowardice that clings,
And stiffness and the soul's arrest:
And feed my brain with better things.
GILBERT KEITH CHESTERTON

Without ambition one starts nothing. Without work one finishes nothing. The prize will not be sent to you. You have to win it.
—RALPH WALDO EMERSON

May 30

Where you die, I will die.
RUTH 1:17

Though Love repine, and Reason chafe,
There came a voice without reply,—
'Tis man's perdition to be safe,
When for the truth he ought to die.
RALPH WALDO EMERSON

Here begins the open sea. Here begins the glorious adventure, the only one abreast with human curiosity, the only one that soars as high as its highest longing. Let us accustom ourselves to regard death as a form of life which we do not yet understand; let us learn to look upon it with the same eye that looks upon birth; and soon our mind will be accompanied to the steps of the tomb with the same glad expectation as greets a birth.

—MAURICE MAETERLINCK

May 31

He makes me lie down in green pastures.
PSALMS 23:2

I can hear these violets chorus
To the sky's benediction above;
And we all are together lying
On the bosom of Infinite Love.

Oh, the peace at the heart of Nature!
Oh, the light that is not of day!
Why seek it afar forever,
When it cannot be lifted away?
W. C. GANNETT

The best remedy for those who are afraid, lonely or unhappy is to go outside, somewhere where they can be quite alone with the heavens, nature and God. Because only then does one feel that all is as it should be and that God wishes to see people happy, amidst the simple beauty of nature. As longs as this exists, and it certainly always will, I know that then there will always be comfort for every sorrow, whatever the circumstances may be. And I firmly believe that nature brings solace in all troubles.

—ANNE FRANK

Those who contemplate the beauty of the earth find reserves of strength that will endure as long as life lasts. There is something infinitely healing in the repeated refrains of nature—the assurance that dawn comes after night, and spring after winter.

—RACHEL CARSON

June

June 1

Even the sparrow has found a home,
and the swallow a nest for herself,
where she may have her young—a place near your altar.
PSALMS 84:3

Our birth is but a sleep and forgetting:
The soul that rises with us, our life's star,
Hath had elsewhere its setting,
And cometh from afar:
Not in entire forgetfulness,
And not in utter nakedness,
But trailing clouds of glory do we come
From God, who is our home . . . .
WILLIAM WORDSWORTH

Home is the place where, when you have to go there,
they have to take you in.

—ROBERT FROST

June 2

Then God said,
"Let us make men in our image, in our likeness . . ."
GENESIS 1:26

Then every tempting form of sin,
Shamed in Thy presence, disappears,
And all the glowing, raptured soul
The likeness it contemplates wears.
P. DODDRIDGE

A human being is a part of the whole called by us universe, a part limited in time and space. He experiences himself, his thoughts and feeling as something separated from the rest, a kind of optical delusion of his consciousness. This delusion is a kind of prison for us, restricting us to our personal desires and to affection for a few persons nearest to us. Our task must be to free ourselves from this prison by widening our circle of compassion to embrace all living creatures and the whole of nature in its beauty.

—ALBERT EINSTEIN

June 3

A cheerful heart is good medicine,
but a crushed spirit dries up the bones.
PROVERBS 17:22

If you have only one smile in you, give it to the people you love. Don't be surly at home, then go out in the street and start grinning 'Good morning' at total strangers.

—MAYA ANGELOU

Cultivate an attitude of happiness. Cultivate a spirit of optimism. Walk with faith, rejoicing in the beauties of nature, in the goodness of those you love, in the testimony which you carry in your heart concerning things divine.

—GORDON B. HINKLEY

June 4

*God is not unjust; he will not forget your work and the love you
have shown him as you have helped his people and continue to
help them. We want each of you to show this same diligence to the very
end, in order to make your hope sure. We do not want
you to become lazy, but to imitate those who through faith and patience
inherit what has been promised.*

HEBREWS 6:10-12

Say not, 'Twas all in vain,
The anguish and the darkness and the strife;
Love thrown upon the waters comes again
In quenchless yearnings for a nobler life.

ANNA SHIPTON

To whatever world death introduce you, the best conceivable
preparation for it is to labor for the highest good of the world in
which you live. Be the change which death brings what it may, he
who has spent his life in trying to make this world better can never
be unprepared for another. If heaven is for the pure and holy, if that
which makes men good is that which best qualifies for heaven,
what better discipline in goodness can we conceive for a human
spirit . . . than to live and labor for a brother's welfare? To find our
deepest joy, not in the delights of sense, nor in the gratification of
personal ambition, nor even in the serene pursuits of culture and
science—nay, not even in seeking the safety of our own souls, but
in striving for the highest good of those who are dear to our Father
in heaven, and the moral and spiritual redemption of that world for
which the Son of God lived and died—say, can a nobler school of
goodness be discovered than this? Where shall love and sympathy
and beneficence find ampler training, or patience, courage,

dauntless devotion, nobler opportunities of exercise, than in the war with evil? . . . Live in this, find your dearest work here, let love to God and man be the animating principle of your being; and then, let death come when it may, and carry you where it will, you will not be unprepared for it . . . for you cannot in God's universe go where love and truth and self-devotion are things of naught, or where a soul, filled with undying faith in the progress and identifying its own happiness with the final triumph of goodness, shall find itself forsaken.

—JOHN CAIRD

June 5

. . . and that you may love the Lord your God, listen to his voice and hold fast to him.
DEUTERONOMY 30:20

I have just hung up; why did he telephone?
I don't know . . . Oh! I get it . . .
I talked a lot and listened very little.

Forgive me, Lord, it was a monologue and not a dialogue.
I explained my idea and did not get his;
Since I didn't listen, I learned nothing,
Since I didn't listen, I didn't help,
Since I didn't listen, we didn't communicate.

Forgive me, Lord, for we were connected,
and now we are cut off.
MICHEL QUOIST

Remember to hold hands and cherish the moment for someday that person might not be there again. Give time to love, give time to speak! And give time to share the precious thoughts in your mind.

—BOB MOOREHEAD

June 6

---

*And in him you too are being built together
to become a dwelling in which
God lives by his Spirit.*
EPHESIANS 2:22

Slowly, through all the universe, that temple of God is being built. Wherever, in any world, a soul, by free-willed obedience, catches the fire of God's likeness, it is set into the growing walls, a living stone. When, in your hard fight, in your tiresome drudgery, or in your terrible temptation, you catch the purpose of your being, and give yourself to God, and so give Him the chance to give Himself to you, your life, a living stone, is taken up and set into that growing wall. . . . Wherever souls are being tried and ripened, in whatever commonplace and homely ways—there God is hewing out the pillars for His temple.

—PHILLIPS BROOKS

The people walking in darkness have seen a great light;
on those living in the land of the shadow of death a light has dawned.
ISAIAH 9:2

Blessed are those who have learned to acclaim you,
who walk in the light of your presence, O Lord.
PSALMS 89:15

O God, who broughtest me from the rest of last night
Unto the joyous light of this day,
Be thou bringing me from the new light of this day
Unto the guiding light of eternity.
Oh! from the new light of this day
Unto the guiding light of eternity.
CARMINA GADELICA

Darkness cannot drive out darkness: only light can do that. Hate
cannot drive out hate: only love can do that.

—MARTIN LUTHER KING, JR.

All the darkness in the world cannot extinguish the light of a
single candle.

—ST. FRANCIS OF ASSISI

June 8

Let the little children come to me, and do not hinder them,
for the kingdom of God belongs to such as these.
LUKE 18:16

> *He prayeth best who loveth best*
> *All things both great and small;*
> *For the dear God who loveth us,*
> *He made and loveth all.*
SAMUEL TAYLOR COLERIDGE

> *In small proportions we just beauties see,*
> *And in short measures life may perfect be.*
BEN JOHNSON

Wisdom comes . . . not from trying to do great things for God . . . but more from being faithful to the small, obscure tasks few people ever see.

—CHARLES R. SWINDOLL

Love's secret is to be always doing things for God, and not to mind because they are such very little ones.

—F. W. FABER

June 9

An angry man stirs up dissension,
and a hot-tempered one commits many sins.
PROVERBS 29:22

Everyone should be quick to listen,
slow to speak and slow to become angry, for man's anger
does not bring about the righteous life that God desires.
JAMES 1:19-20

Let this truth be present to thee in the excitement of anger—
that to be moved by passion is not manly, but that mildness and
gentleness, as they are more agreeable to human nature, so also
are they more manly. . . . For in the same degree in which a man's
mind is nearer to freedom from all passion, in the same degree also
is it nearer to strength.

—MARCUS ANTONINUS

Anger is a short madness.

—HORACE

Anger is a weed, hate is the tree.

—ST. AUGUSTINE

June 10

You, O lord, keep my lamp burning;
my god turns my darkness into light.
PSALMS 18:28

When we in darkness walk,
Nor feel the heavenly flame,
Then is the time to trust our God,
And rest upon His name.

A. M. TOPLADY

There is hardly a man or woman in the world who has not got some corner of self into which he or she fears to venture with a light. The reasons for this may be various, as various as the individual souls. Nevertheless, in spite of the variety of reasons, the fact is universal. For the most part we hardly know our own reasons. It is an instinct, one of the quick instincts of corrupt nature. We prophesy to ourselves that, if we penetrate into that corner of self, something will have to be done which either our laziness or our immortification would shrink from doing. If we enter that sanctuary, some charm of easy devotion or smooth living will be broken. We shall find ourselves face to face with something unpleasant, something which will perhaps constrain us to all the trouble and annoyance of a complete interior revolution, or else leave us very uncomfortable in conscience. . . . So we leave this corner of self curtained off, locked up like a room in a house with disagreeable associations attached to it, unvisited like a lumber closet where we are conscious that disorder and dirt are accumulating, which we have not just now the vigor to grapple with. But do we think that God cannot enter there except by our unlocking the door? Or see anything when He is there, unless we hold Him a light? . . . We know how His eye rests upon us incessantly, and takes us all in, and searches us out, and as it were burns us up with His holy gaze. His perfections environ us with the most awful nearness, flooding us with insupportable light. . . . to be straightforward with God is neither an easy nor a common grace. O with what unutterable faith must we believe in our own falsehood, when we can feel it to be anything like a shelter in the presence of the all-seeing God!

—FREDERICK WILLIAM FABER

June 11

When I called, you answered me;
you made me bold and stouthearted.
PSALMS 138:3

Ask and it will be given to you . . .
LUKE 11:9

Lord, one thing we want,
More holiness grant;
For more of thy mind and thy image we pant
While onward we move
To Canaan above,
Come, fill us with holiness, fill us with love.
ANONYMOUS

There is only one important point you must keep in your mind and let it be your guide. No matter what people call you, you are just who you are. Keep to this truth. You must ask yourself how is it you want to live your life. We live and we die, this is the truth that we can only face alone. No one can help us, not even the Buddha. So consider carefully, what prevents you from living the way you want to live your life?

—DALAI LAMA XIV

It is faith's work to claim and challenge loving-kindness out of all
the roughest strokes of God.

—S. RUTHERFORD

June 12

I have fought the good fight, I have finished the race,
I have kept the faith. Now there is in store for me the crown
of righteousness, which the Lord, the righteous Judge,
will award to me on that day . . .
2 TIMOTHY 4:7-8

We listened to a man whom we felt to be, with all his heart
and soul and strength, striving against whatever was mean and
unmanly and unrighteous in our little world. It was not the cold
clear voice of one giving advice and warning from serene heights
to those who were struggling and sinning below, but the warm
living voice of one who was fighting for us and by our sides, and
calling on us to help him and ourselves and one another. And so,
wearily and little by little, but surely and steadily on the whole, was
brought home to the young boy, for the first time, the meaning of
his life; that it was no fool's or sluggard's paradise into which he
had wandered by chance, but a battle-field ordained from of old,
where there are no spectators, but the youngest must take his side,
and the stakes are life and death.

—THOMAS HUGHES

June 13

Your word is a lamp to my feet and a light for my path.
PSALMS 119:105

> *Lead, kindly Light, amid the encircling gloom;*
> *Lead thou me on!*
> *The night is dark, and I am far from home;*
> *Lead thou me on!*
> *Keep thou my feet: I do not ask to see*
> *The distant scene; one step enough for me.*
> JOHN HENRY CARDINAL NEWMAN

Thus out of small beginnings greater things have been produced by His hand that made all things of nothing, and give being too all things that are; and, as one small candle may light a thousand, so the light here kindled hath shone unto many, yea in some sort to our whole nation.

—WILLIAM BRADFORD

June 14

On the day the Lord gives you relief from suffering
and turmoil and cruel bondage . . .
ISAIAH 14:3

Stilled now be every anxious care
See God's great goodness everywhere
Leave all to Him in perfect rest:
He will do all things for the best.
ANONYMOUS

O Lord, support us all the day long, until the shadows lengthen and the evening comes, and the busy world is hushed, and the fever of life is over, and our work is done. Then in thy mercy grant us a safe lodging, and a holy rest, and peace at the last.

—JOHN HENRY CARDINAL NEWMAN

When we are tired, we are attacked by ideas we conquered long ago.

—FRIEDRICH NIETZSCHE

June 15

The fear of the Lord teaches a man wisdom,
and humility comes before honor.
PROVERBS 15:33

The only wisdom we can hope to acquire
Is the wisdom of humility: humility is endless.
T. S. ELIOT

" . . . there's nothing so becomes a man
As modest stillness and humility . . . "
WILLIAM SHAKESPEARE

Because God is never cruel, there is a reason for all things. We must know the pain of loss; because if we never knew it, we would have no compassion for others, and we would become monsters of self-regard, creatures of unalloyed self-interest. The terrible pain of loss teaches humility to our prideful kind, has the power to soften uncaring hearts, to make a better person of a good one.

—DEAN KOOTZ

June 16

Great and marvelous are your deeds, Lord God Almighty.
Just and true are your ways, King of the ages.
REVELATIONS 15:3-4

A pessimist is one who makes difficulties of his opportunities and an optimist is one who makes opportunities of his difficulties.

—HARRY TRUMAN

It's not what's happening to you now or what has happened in your past that determines who you become. Rather, it's your decisions about what to focus on, what things mean to you, and what you're going to do about them that will determine your ultimate destiny.

—ANTHONY ROBBINS

June 17

The righteous will flourish like a palm tree,
they will grow like a cedar of Lebanon . . .
PSALMS 92:12

See how the lilies of the field grow, they do not labor or spin.
MATTHEW 6:28

How shall we sing our love's song now
In this strange land where all are born to die?
Each tree and leaf and star show how
The universe is part of this one cry,
Every life is noted and is cherished,
and nothing loved is ever lost or perished.
MADELEINE L'ENGLE

We are all affecting the world every moment, whether we mean to or not. Our actions and states of mind matter, because we are so deeply interconnected with one another.

—RAM DASS

Thine own self-will and anxiety, thy hurry and labor, disturb thy peace and prevent Me from working in thee. Look at the little flowers, in the serene summer days; they quietly open their petals, and the sun shines into them with his gentle influences. So will I do for thee, if thou wilt yield thyself to Me.

—G. TERSTEEGEN

June 18

And do not set your heart on what you will eat or drink;
do not worry about it.
LUKE 12:29

If that is how God clothes the grass of the field, which is here today
and tomorrow is thrown into the fire, will he not much more clothe you,
O you of little faith?
MATTHEW 6:30

> They do not toil:
> Content with their allotted task
> They do but grow; they do not ask
> A richer lot, a higher sphere,
> But in their loveliness appear,
> And grow, and smile, and do their best,
> And unto God they leave the rest.

MARIANNE FARNINGHAM

There are people in the world so hungry, that God cannot appear to
them except in the form of bread.

—MAHATMA GANDHI

June 19

The Lord watches over you—
the Lord is your shade at your right hand.
PSALMS 121:5

Under Thy wings, my God, I rest,
Under Thy shadow safety lie;
By Thy own strength in peace possessed,
While dreaded evils pass me by.
A. L. WARING

The Road goes ever on and on
Out from the door where it began.
Now far ahead the Road has gone.
Let others follow, if they can!
Let them a journey new begin.
But I at last with weary feet
Will turn towards the lighted inn,
My evening-rest and sleep to meet.
J.R.R. TOLKIEN

June 20

The eternal God is your refuge . . . .
DEUTRONOMY 33:27

A ship is safe in harbor, but that's not what ships are for.
—WILLIAM G.T. SHEDD

In vain will you let your mind run out after help in times of trouble; it is like putting to sea in a storm. Sit still, and feel after your principles; and, if you find none that furnish you with somewhat of a stay and prop, and which point you to quietness and silent submission, depend upon it you have never yet learned Truth from the Spirit of Truth, whatever notions thereof you may have picked up from this and the other description of it.

—M. A. KELTY

June 21

I have strayed like a lost sheep . . . .
PSALMS 119:176

There is no path to happiness: happiness is the path.
SIDDHARTHA GAUTAMA

When you find your path, you must not be afraid. You need to have sufficient courage to make mistakes. Disappointment, defeat, and despair are the tools God uses to show us the way.

—PAULO COELHO

June 22

. . . weeping may remain for a night,
but rejoicing comes in the morning.
PSALMS 30:5

Every morning we are born again.
What we do today is what matters most.
SIDDHARTHA GAUTAMA

Everything which happens, either happens in such wise that thou art formed by nature to bear it, or that thou art not formed, by nature to bear it. If then, it happens to thee in such way that thou art formed by nature to bear it, do not complain, but bear it as thou art formed by nature to bear it. But, if it happens in such wise that thou art not able to bear it, do not complain; for it will perish after it has consumed thee. Remember, however, that thou art formed by nature to bear everything, with respect to which it depends on thy own opinion to make it endurable and tolerable, by thinking that it is either thy interest or thy duty to do this.

—MARCUS ANTONINUS

June 23

Why are you downcast, O my soul?
Why so disturbed within me?
Put your hope in God,
for I will yet praise him, my savior and my God.

PSALMS 42:11

I Praise Thee while my days go on;
I love Thee while my days go on:
Through dark and dearth, through fire and frost,
With emptied arms and treasure lost,
I thank Thee while my days go on.

ELIZABETH BARRETT BROWNING

You may encounter many defeats, but you must not be defeated. In fact, it may be necessary to encounter the defeats, so you can know who you are, what you can rise from, how you can still come out of it.

—MAYA ANGELOU

June 24

This is the way; walk in it.

ISAIAH 30:21

O Jesus
Be the canoe that holds me in the sea of life.
Be the steer that keeps me straight.
Be the outrigger that supports me in times of great temptation.
Let thy spirit be my sail that carries me through each day.
Keep my body strong,
so that I may paddle steadfastly on,
in the long voyage of life.
A NEW HEBRIDEAN PRAYER

Most of us die of something; of disease, accident, old age. But occasionally there appears in our midst a man who resolves to die for something, like Winkelried when he gathered the spears of the Austrians into his breast at the battle of Sempach. This dying for something, instead of waiting to die of something, as most of us do, this deliberate dying for something deemed worthy of it, is the strongest form of self-affirmation I know of. The power and vitality of it are tremendous, and the stamp that it leaves on the world is indelible. The Christian religion is an example of it.

—L. P. JACKS

June 25

I desire to do your will,
O my God; your law is in my heart.

PSALMS 40:8

God wills us free, man wills us slaves,
I will as God wills, God's will be done.

DANIEL BLISS

We mustn't be in a hurry to fix and choose our own lot; we must wait to be guided. We are led on, like the little children, by a way that we know not. It is a vain thought to flee from the work that God appoints us, for the sake of finding a greater blessing to our own souls; as if we could choose for ourselves where we shall find the fullness of the Divine Presence, instead of seeking it where alone it is to be found, in loving obedience.

—GEORGE ELIOT

June 26

There is not a righteous man on earth
who does what is right and never sins.

ECCLESIASTES 7:20

For thou lovest all the things that are,
And abhorrest nothing which thou hast made:
For never wouldst thou have made anything if thou hadst hated it.
And how could anything have endured,
If it had not been thy Will?
Or been preserved, if not called by Thee?
But thou sparest all:
For they are thine,
O Lord, Thou lover of souls.
WISDOM OF SOLOMON 11:24-26

You don't love someone because they're perfect, you love them in spite of the fact that they're not. . .

—JODI PICULT

June 27

Create in me a pure heart,
O God, and renew a steadfast spirit within me.
PSALMS 51:10

Think what Spirit dwells within thee;
Think what Father's smiles are thine;
Think that Jesus died to win thee:
Child of heaven, canst thou repine?
ANONYMOUS

When you close your doors, and make darkness within, remember never to say that you are alone, for you are not alone; nay, God is within, and your genius is within. And what need have they of light to see what you are doing?

—EPICTETUS

Then does a good man become the tabernacle of God, wherein the divine Shechinah does rest, and which the divine glory fills, when the frame of his mind and life is wholly according to that idea and pattern which he receives from the mount.

—DR. JOHN SMITH

June 28

. . . doing what is right and just and fair:
for giving prudence to the simple . . .
PROVERBS 1:3-4

The Lord protects the simple-hearted . . .
PSALMS 116:6

'Tis the gift to be simple,
'Tis the gift to be free,
'Tis the gift to come down
Where we ought to be.
SHAKER SONG

This deliverance of the soul from all useless and selfish and unquiet cares, brings to it an unspeakable peace and freedom; this is true simplicity. This state of entire resignation and perpetual acquiescence produces true liberty; and this liberty brings perfect simplicity. The soul which knows no self-seeking, no interested ends, is thoroughly candid; it goes straight forward without hindrance; its path opens daily more and more to 'perfect day', in proportion as its self-renunciation and its self-forgetfulness increase; and its peace, amid whatever troubles beset it, will be as boundless as the depths of the sea.

—FENELON

June 29

The Lord is the strength and my shield;
my heart trusts in him, and I am helped.
My heart leaps for joy and
I will give thanks to him in song.
PSALMS 28:7

No coward soul is mine,
No trembler in the world's storm-troubled sphere:
I see Heaven's glories shine,
And faith shines equal, arming me from fear.

O God within my breast,
Almighty, ever-present Deity!
Life—that in me has rest,
As I—undying Life—have power in Thee!
EMILY BRONTE

The humblest citizen of all the land, when clad in the armor of a righteous cause, is stronger than all the hosts of Error.

—WILLIAM JENNINGS BRYAN

Your faith is only as strong as the tests it survives. How strong are you? Strength must be tested before it can be considered reliable.

—MYLES MONROE

June 30

But for you who revere my name, the sun of righteousness will rise with healing in its wings. And you will go out and leap like calves released from the stall.

MALACHI 4:2

To love. To be loved. To never forget your own insignificance. To never get used to the unspeakable violence and the vulgar disparity of life around you. To seek joy in the saddest places. To pursue beauty to its lair. To never simplify what is complicated or complicate what is simple. To respect strength, never power. Above all, to watch. To try and understand. To never look away. And never, never, to forget.

—ARUNDHATI ROY

July

July 1

. . . and in the morning you will see the glory of the Lord.
EXODUS 16:7

Every day is a fresh beginning,
Every morn is the world made new.
You who are weary of sorrow and sinning,
Here is a beautiful hope for you;
A hope for me and a hope for you.
SUSAN COLLIDGE

Be patient with every one, but above all with yourself. I mean, do not be disturbed because of your imperfections, and always rise up bravely from a fall. I am glad that you make a daily new beginning; there is no better means of progress in the spiritual life than to be continually beginning afresh, and never to think that we have done enough.

—ST. FRANCIS DE SALES

Because perseverance is so difficult, even when supported by the grace of God, thence is the value of new beginnings. For new beginnings are the life of perseverance.

—E. B. PUSEY

July 2

I will instruct you and teach you in the way you should go;
I will counsel you and watch over you.

PSALM 32:8

Oh, keep thy conscience sensitive;
No inward token miss;
And go where grace entices thee;
Perfection lies in this.

F. W. FABER

Every man is represented as having a kind of court and tribunal
in his own breast; where he tries himself and all his actions,
and conscience, under one notion or another, sustains all parts
in this trial. The court is called the court of a man's conscience,
and the bar at which the sinner stands impleaded is called the
bar of conscience. Conscience also is the accuser, and it is the
record and the register of our crimes, in which the memory of
them is preserved; and it is the witness which gives testimony
for or against us; hence are those expressions of the testimony
of our consciences, and that a man's own conscience is to him,
instead of a thousand witnesses. And it is likewise the judge which
declares the law, and what we ought or ought not to have done, in
such or such a case, and accordingly passes sentence upon us by
acquitting or condemning us . . . . Hence we should reverence our
consciences and stand in awe of them, and have a great regard to
their testimony and verdict. For conscience is a domestic judge, and
kind of a familiar god; and therefore next to the supreme Majesty
of heaven and earth, every man should be afraid to offend his own
reason and conscience which, whenever we knowingly do amiss,
will beat us with many stripes and handle us more severely than
the greatest enemy we have in the world . . . . The most sensual

man that ever was in the world never felt his heart touched with so delicious and lasting a pleasure as that is which springs from a clear conscience and a mind fully satisfied with his own actions.

This makes all calm and serene within, when there is nothing but clouds and darkness about him.

—JOHN TILLOTSON

July 3

Joshua said to them, "Do not be afraid; do not be discouraged. Be strong and courageous. This is what the Lord will do to all the enemies you are going to fight."
JOSHUA 10: 25

In the depth of winter, I finally learned that within me there lay an invincible summer.
ALBERT CAMUS

You gain strength, courage, and confidence by every experience in which you really stop to look fear in the face. You are able to say to yourself, "I have lived through this horror. I can take the next thing that comes along." You must do the thing you think you cannot do.

—ELEANOR ROOSEVELT

July 4

Remember,
O Lord, your great mercy and love,
for they are from old.
PSALMS 25:6

Though much is taken, much abides; and though
We are not now that strength which in old days
Moved earth and heaven, that which we are, we are;
One equal temper of heroic hearts,
Made weak by time and fate, but strong in will
To strive, to seek, to find, and not to yield.
LORD ALFRED TENNYSON

The truth is, part of me is every age. I'm a three-year-old, I'm a
five-year-old, I'm a thirty-seven-year-old, I'm a fifty-year-old. I've
been through all of them, and I know what it's like. I delight in
being a child when it's appropriate to be a child. I delight in being a
wise old man when it's appropriate to be a wise old man. Think of
all I can be! I am every age, up to my own.

—MITCH ALBOM

July 5

A bruised reed he will not break,
and a smoldering wick he will not snuff out.
PSALMS 42:3

Dear God, be good to me;
The sea is so wide,
And my boat is so small.
BRETON FISHERMEN'S PRAYER

Being thus arrived in a good harbor, and brought safe to land, they fell upon their knees and the God of Heaven who had brought them over the vast and furious ocean, and delivered them from all the perils and miseries thereof, again to set their feet on the firm and stable earth, their proper element.

—WILLIAM BRADFORD

July 6

The gracious hand of our God is on everyone who looks to him, but his great anger is against all who forsake him.
EZRA 8:22

I do not ask my cross to understand,
My ways to see;
Better in darkness just to feel Thy hand,
And follow Thee.
ADELAIDE A. PROCTER

If you and I are having a single thought of violence or hatred against anyone in the world at this moment, we are contributing to the wounding of the world.

—DEEPAK CHOPRA

July 7

The Lord is my light and my salvation—
whom shall I fear?
The Lord is the stronghold of my life—
of whom shall I be afraid?

PSALMS 27:1

He will complete the work begun
He will his own defend;
Will give me strength my course to run,
And, love me to the end.

ANONYMOUS

High hearts are never long without hearing some new call, some distant clarion of God, even in their dreams; and soon they are observed to break up the camp of ease, and start on some fresh march of faithful service. And, looking higher still, we find those who never wait till their moral work accumulates, and who reward resolution with no rest; with whom, therefore, the alternation is instantaneous and constant; who do the good only to see the better, and see the better only to achieve it; who are too meek for transport, too faithful for remorse, too earnest for repose; whose worship is action and whose action ceaseless aspiration.

—J. MARTINEAU

Speak up for those who cannot speak for themselves,
for the rights of all who are destitute.
Speak up and judge fairly;
defend the rights of the poor and needy.
PROVERBS 31:8-9

If I can stop one Heart from breaking
I shall not live in vain
If I can ease one Life the Aching
Or cool one pain
Or help one fainting Robin
Unto his Nest again
I shall not live in Vain.
EMILY DICKENSON

We may, if we choose, make the worst of one another. Every one has his weak points; every one has his faults; we may make the worst of these; we may fix our attention constantly upon these. But we may also make the best of one another. We may forgive, even as we hope to be forgiven. We may put ourselves in the place of others, and ask what we should wish to be done to us, and thought of us, were we in their place. By loving whatever is lovable in those around us, love will flow back from them to us, and life will become a pleasure instead of a pain; and earth will become like heaven; and we shall become not unworthy followers of Him whose name is Love.

—A. P. STANLEY

July 9

Bear with each other and forgive whatever grievances you may have against one another. Forgive as the Lord forgave you.
COLOSSIANS 3:13

Life is short, Break the rules.
Forgive quickly, Kiss slowly.
Love truly. Laugh uncontrollably
And never regret anything
That makes you smile.
MARK TWAIN

Holding on to anger is like grasping a hot coal with the intent of throwing it at someone else; you are the one who gets burned.
—SIDDHARTHA GAUTAMA

July 10

He . . . must work, doing something useful with his own hands . . .
EPHESIANS 4:28

. . . May he bless all who build the bridge,
and keep them faithful and safe in their work.

May the peoples of this city be united and godfearing,
happy and prosperous,
preserving the good heritage of the past,
and building the future on foundations of
righteousness and love.

G. A.

Human felicity is produced not so much by great pieces of good fortune that seldom happen, as by little advantages that occur every day.

When men are employed, they are best contented; for on the days they worked they were good-natured and cheerful, and, with the consciousness of having done a good day's work, they spent the evening jollily; but on our idle days they were mutinous and quarrelsome.

—BENJAMIN FRANKLIN

July 11

Better a dry crust with peace and quiet,
than a house full
of feasting with strife.
PROVERBS 17:1

Calm Soul of all things! make it mine
To feel, amid the city's jar,
That there bides a peace of thine,
Man did not make, and can not mar.
MATTHEW ARNOLD

When I chased after money, I never had enough. When I got my life on purpose and focused on giving of myself and everything that arrived into my life, then I was prosperous.

—WAYNE DYER

July 12

Be strong and courageous. Do not be afraid or terrified because of them, for the Lord your God goes with you; he will never leave you nor forsake you.
DEUTERONOMY 31:6

Stay with me, God. The night is dark,
The night is cold: my little spark
Of courage dies. The night is long;
Be with me, God, and make me strong.
ANONYMOUS SOLDIER

If people bring so much courage to this world the world has to kill them to break them, so of course it kills them. The world breaks every one and afterward many are strong at the broken places. But those that will not break it kills. It kills the very good and the very gentle and the very brave impartially. If you are none of these you can be sure it will kill you too but there will be no special hurry.

—ERNEST HEMINGWAY

July 13

His God instructs him and teaches him the right way.
ISAIAH 28:26

*The secret of health for both mind and body is not to mourn for
the past, nor to worry about the future, but to live the present
moment wisely and earnestly.*
SIDDHARTHA GAUTAMA

Lord, I thank you for teaching me how to live in the present
moment. In this way I enjoy each simple task as I do it without
thinking that I must hurry on to the next thing. I do what I am
doing with all my ability and all my concentration. My mind is no
longer divided, and life is more peaceful. Thank you for teaching
me how to do this, and please help me how to show others the way
to learn to trust you more completely and to do everything which
has to be done at your time and your speed.

—MICHAEL HOLLINGS AND ETTA GULLICK

July 14

*Command those who are rich in this present world not to be arrogant
nor to put their hope in wealth, which is so uncertain, but to put their
hope in God, who richly provides us with everything for our enjoyment.*
1 TIMOTHY 6:17

Do not conform any longer to the pattern of this world,
but be transformed by the renewing of your mind.
ROMANS 12:2

You cannot help the poor by destroying the rich.
You cannot strengthen the weak by weakening the strong.
You cannot bring about prosperity by discouraging thrift.
You cannot lift the wage earner up by pulling the wage payer down.
You cannot further the brotherhood of man by inciting class hatred.
You cannot build character and courage by taking away men's
initiative and independence.
You cannot help men permanently by doing for them, what they
could and should do for themselves.
WILLIAM J.H. BOETCKER

Knowing others is intelligence; knowing yourself is true wisdom.
Mastering others is strength; mastering yourself is true power. If
you realize that you have enough, you are truly rich.

—LAO TZU

July 15

Now you have been pleased to bless the house of your servant,
that it may continue forever in your sight;
for you, O Lord, have blessed it,
and it will be blessed forever.

1 CHRONICLES 17:27

"God bless us every one!" said Tiny Tim, the last of all.

—CHARLES DICKENS

Work is a blessing. God has so arranged the world that work
is necessary, and He gives us hands and strength to do it. The
enjoyment of leisure would be nothing if we had only leisure. It is
the joy of work well done that enables us to enjoy rest, just as it
is the experiences of hunger and thirst that make food and drink
such pleasures.

—ELISABETH ELLIOT

July 16

Then my head will be exalted above the enemies who surround me;
at his tabernacle will I sacrifice with shouts of joy;
I will sing and make music to the Lord.

PSALMS 27:6

Let us be grateful to the people who make us happy; they are the charming gardeners who make our souls blossom.
MARCEL PROUST

Cultivate the habit of being grateful for every good thing that comes to you, and to give thanks continuously. And because all things have contributed to your advancement, you should include all things in your gratitude.

—RALPH WALDO EMERSON

July 17

*For great is your love toward me;
you have delivered me from the depths of the grave.*
PSALMS 86:13

"No man ever saw God and lived"; and yet I shall not live till I see God; and when I have seen Him I shall never die. What have I ever seen in this world that hath been truly the same thing that it seemed to me? I have seen marble buildings, and a chip, a crust, a plaster, a face of marble hath peeled off, and I see brick-bowels within. I have seen beauty, and a strong breath from another tells me that complexion is from without, not from a sound constitution within. I have seen the state of princes, and all that is but ceremony; and I would be loath to put a master of ceremonies to define ceremony and tell me what it is, and to include so various a thing as ceremony in so constant a thing as a definition. I see a great officer, and I see a man of mine own profession, of great revenues, and I see not the interest of the money that was paid for it, I see not the pensions nor the annuities that are charged upon that office or that church. As he that fears God fears nothing else, so he that sees God sees everything else. When we shall see God *sicuti est*, as He is, we shall see all things *sicuti sunt*, as they are; for that's their essence, as they conduce to His glory. We shall be no more deluded with outward appearances: for when this sight which we intend here comes, there will be no delusory thing to be seen. All that we have made as though we saw in this world will be vanished, and I shall see nothing but God, and what is in Him.

—JOHN DONNE

July 18

"I am as you are, my people as your people,
my horses as your horses."
1 KINGS 22:4

She doeth little kindnesses
Which most leave undone or despise
For nought which sets one heart at ease,
And giveth happiness or peace,
Is low-esteemed in her eyes.
J. R. LOWELL

Do anything you can do to keep your mind off yourself. Purposefully be a blessing to someone else today.

—JOYCE MEYERS

The remarkable thing is that we really love our neighbor as ourselves: we do unto others as we do unto ourselves. We hate others when we hate ourselves. We are tolerant toward others when we tolerate ourselves. We forgive others when we forgive ourselves. We are prone to sacrifice others when we are ready to sacrifice ourselves.

—ERIC HOFFLER

July 19

*For everything God created is good,
and nothing is to be rejected if it is received with thanksgiving,
because it is consecrated by the word of God and prayer.*
1 TIMOTHY 4:4

*To see a world in a grain of sand
And heaven in a wild flower,
Hold infinity in the palm of your hand
And eternity in and hour.*
WILLIAM BLAKE

The sun shines down, and its image reflects in a thousand different pots filled with water. The reflections are many, but they are each reflecting the same sun. Similarly, when we come to know who we truly are, we will see ourselves in all people.

—MATA AMRITANANDAMAYI DEVI

I would give nothing for that man's religion whose very dog and cat are not the better for it.

—ROWLAND HILL

July 20

. . . they will wear themselves out but gain nothing.
JEREMIAH 12:13

Unless the Lord builds the house, its builders labor in vain.
PSALMS 127:1

If the people about you are carrying on their business or their benevolence at a pace which drains the life out of you, resolutely take a slower pace; be called a laggard, make less money, accomplish less work than they, but be what you were meant to be and can be. You have your natural limit of power as much as an engine—ten-horse power, or twenty, or a hundred. You are fit to do certain kinds of work, and you need a certain kind and amount of fuel, and a certain kind of handling.

—GEORGE S. MERRIAM

In your occupations, try to possess your soul in peace. It is not a good plan to be in haste to perform any action that it may be the sooner over. On the contrary, you should accustom yourself to do whatever you have to do with tranquility, in order that you may retain the possession of yourself and of settled peace.

—MADAME GUYON

Therefore we do not lose heart. Though outwardly we are wasting away, yet inwardly we are being renewed day by day.
2 CORINTHIANS 4:16

And now in age I bud again,
After so many deaths I live and write;
I once more smell the dew and rain,
And relish versing: O my only light,
It cannot be
That I am he
On whom thy tempests fell all night.
GEORGE HERBERT

In my attempts to promote the comfort of my family, the quiet of my spirit has been disturbed. Some of this is doubtless owing to physical weakness; but, with every temptation, there is a way of escape; there is never any need to sin. Another thing I have suffered loss from—entering into the business of the day without seeking to have my spirit quieted and directed. So many things press upon me, this is sometimes neglected shame to me that it should be so.

This is of great importance, to watch carefully—now I am so weak—not to over-fatigue myself, because then I cannot contribute to the pleasure of others; and a placid face and a gentle tone will make my family more happy than anything else I can do for them. Our own will gets sadly into the performance of our duties sometimes.

—ELIZABETH T. KING

July 22

He is good; His love endures forever.
2 CHRONICLES 5:13

The one remains, the many change and pass;
Heaven's light forever shines, earth's shadows fly;
Life, like a dome of many-colored glass,
Stains the white radiance of eternity,
Until Death tramples it to fragments—Die,
If thou wouldst be with that which thou dost seek.
PERCY BYSSHE SHELLEY

The only way love can last a lifetime is if it's unconditional. The truth is this: love is not determined by the one being loved but rather by the one choosing to love.

—STEPHEN KENDRICK

July 23

Love the Lord your God with all your heart and with all your soul
and with all your strength and with all your mind.
LUKE 10:27

To love God "with all our heart," is to know the spiritual passion of measureless gratitude for loving-kindness, and self-devotedness to goodness; to love Him "with all our mind," is to know the passion for Truth that is the enthusiasm of Science, the passion for Beauty that inspires the poet and the artist, when all truth and beauty are regarded as the self-revealings of God; to love Him "with all our soul," is to know the saint's rapture of devotion and gaze of penitential awe into the face of the All-holy, the saint's abhorrence of sin, and agony of desire to save a sinner's soul and to love Him "with all our strength," is the supreme spiritual passion that tests the rest; the passion for reality, for worship in spirit and in truth, for being what we adore, for doing what we know to be God's word; the loyalty that exacts the living sacrifice, the whole burnt-offering that is our reasonable service, and in our coldest hours keeps steadfast to what seemed good when we were aglow.

—J. H. THOM

July 24

And I pray that you, being rooted and established in love, may have power, together with all the saints, to grasp how wide and long and high and deep is the love of Christ, and to know this love that surpasses knowledge.

EPHESIANS 3:17-19

Accept the place the divine providence has found for you, the society of your contemporaries, the connection of events.

—RALPH WALDO EMERSON

Adapt thyself to the things with which thy lot has been cast; and love the men with whom it is thy portion to live, and that with a sincere affection. . . . No longer be either dissatisfied with thy present lot, or shrink from the future.

—MARCUS ANTINONUS

I love best to have each thing in its season, doing without it at all other times. I have never got over my surprise that I should have been born into the most estimable place in all the world, and in the very nick of time too.

—HENRY DAVID THOREAU

July 25

The light shines in the darkness,
but the darkness has not understood it.
JOHN 1:5

A man's steps are directed by the Lord.
How then can anyone understand his own way?
PROVERBS 20:24

So let the way wind up the hill or down,
O'er rough or smooth, the journey will be joy;
Still seeking what I sought when but a boy,
New friendship, high adventure, and a crown.
My heart will keep the courage of the quest,
And hope the road's last turn will be the best.
HENRY VAN DYKE

But indeed Conviction, were it never so excellent, is worthless till it convert itself into Conduct. Nay properly Conviction is not possible till then; inasmuch as all Speculation is by nature endless, formless, a vortex amid vortices: only by a felt indubitable certainty of Experience does it find any center to revolve round, and so fashion itself into a system. Most true is it, as a wise man teaches us, that "Doubt of any sort cannot be removed except by Action." On which ground, too, let him who gropes painfully in darkness or uncertain light, and prays vehemently that the dawn may ripen into day, lay this other precept well to heart, which to me was of invaluable service: "Do the Duty which lies nearest thee," which thou knowest to be a Duty! Thy second Duty will already have become clearer.

—THOMAS CARLYLE

July 26

But blessed is the man who trusts in the Lord,
whose confidence is in him.

JEREMIAH 17:7

Those who trust in the Lord are like Mount Zion,
which cannot be shaken but endures forever.

PSALMS 125:1

How on a rock they stand,
Who watch His eye, and hold His guiding hand!
Not half so fixed amid her vassal hills,
Rises the holy pile that Kedron's valley fills.

J. KEBLE

As long as you live, you will be subject to change, whether you will it or not—now glad, now sorrowful; now pleased, now displeased; now devout, now undevout; now vigorous, now slothful; now gloomy, now merry. But a wise man who is well taught in spiritual labor stands unshaken in all such things, and heeds little what he feels, or from what side the wind of instability blows.

—THOMAS A KEMPIS

A man who has riches without understanding is
like the beasts that perish.
PSALMS 49:20

. . . for wisdom is more precious than rubies,
and nothing you desire can compare with her.
PROVERBS 8:11

O World, thou choosest not the better part!
It is not wisdom to be only wise,
And on the inward vision close the eyes,
But it is wisdom to believe the heart.
GEORGE SANTAYANA

Knowledge is proud that he has learn'd so much; Wisdom is humble that he knows no more.

—WILLIAM COWPER

To be a philosopher is not merely to have subtle thoughts, nor even to found a school, but so to love wisdom as to live accordingly to its dictates, a life of simplicity, independence, magnanimity and trust.

—HENRY DAVID THOREAU

The wisest man is he that does not fancy that he is so at all.

—NICOLAS BOILEAU-DESPREAUX

I want, by understanding myself, to understand others. I want
to be all that I am capable of becoming . . . This all sounds very
strenuous and serious. But now that I have wrestled with it, it's no
longer so. I feel happy—deep down. All is well.

—KATHERINE MANSFIELD

July 28

Listen, I tell you a mystery:
We will not all sleep, but we will all be changed . . .
1 CORINTHIANS 15:51

Now I lay me down to sleep,
I pray the Lord my soul to keep;
If I should die before I wake,
I pray the Lord my soul to take.
NEW ENGLAND PRIMER

Death be not proud, though some have called thee
Mighty and dreadful, for thou art not so,
For those whom thou think'st thou dost overthrow,
Die not, poor death, nor yet canst thou kill me.
JOHN DONNE

We give back, to you, O God, those whom you gave to us. You did
not lose them when you gave them to us, and we do not lose them
by their return to you. Your dear Son has taught us that life is
eternal and love cannot die. So death is only an horizon, and an
horizon is only the limit of our sight. Open our eyes to see more

clearly, and draw us closer to you that we may know that we are nearer to our loved ones, who are with you. You have told us that you are preparing a place for us: prepare us also for that happy place, that where you are we may also be always, O dear Lord of life and death.

—WILLIAM PENN

July 29

What I mean, brothers, is that the time is short.
1 CORINTHIANS 7:29

Nor love thy life, nor hate; but what thou liv'st
Live well; how long or short permit to Heaven.
JOHN MILTON

Oh, my dear friends, you who are letting miserable misunderstandings run on from year to year, meaning to clear them up some day; you who are keeping wretched quarrels alive because you cannot quite make up your mind that now is the day to sacrifice your pride and kill them; you who are passing men sullenly upon the street, not speaking to them out of some silly spite, and yet knowing that it would fill you with shame and remorse if you heard that one of those men were dead to-morrow morning; you who are letting your neighbor starve, till you hear that he is dying of starvation; or letting your friend's heart ache for a word of appreciation or sympathy, which you mean to give him some day—if you only could know and see and feel, all of a sudden, that "the time is short," how it would break the spell! How you would go instantly and do the thing which you might never have another chance to do.

—PHILLIPS BROOKS

July 30

O my God, I am too ashamed and
disgraced to lift up my face to you my God,
because our sins are higher than our heads and
our guilt has reached to the heavens.
EZRA 9:6

When on my aching, burdened heart
My sins lie heavily,
My pardon speak, new peace impart,
In love remember me.
T. HAWEIS

We need to know that our sins are forgiven. And how shall we know this? By feeling that we have peace with God, by feeling that we are able so to trust in the divine compassion and infinite tenderness of our Father, as to arise and go to Him, whenever we commit sin, and say at once to Him, "Father, I have sinned; forgive me." To know that we are forgiven, it is only necessary to look at our Father's love till it sinks into our heart, to open our soul to Him till He shall pour His love into it; to wait on Him till we find peace, till our conscience no longer torments us, till the weight of responsibility ceases to be an oppressive burden to us, till we can feel that our sins, great as they are, cannot keep us away from our Heavenly Father.

—J. F. CLARKE

July 31

You guide me with your counsel,
and afterward you will take me into glory.
PSALMS 73:24

Before the throne of the Almighty, man will be judged not by his
acts but by his intentions. For God alone reads our hearts.
MAHATMA GANDHI

The great news is that God knows everything about you, both good and bad, and He still loves you and values you unconditionally. God does not always approve of our behavior. He is not pleased when we go against his will, and when we do, we always suffer the consequences and have to work with Him to correct our thoughts, words, actions, or attitudes. And while you should work to improve in the areas where you fall short, nothing you do will ever cause God to love you less...or more. His love is a constant you can depend on.

—JOEL OSTEEN

August

August 1

A man of knowledge uses words with restraint,
and a man of understanding is even-tempered.
PROVERBS 17:27

But, children, you should never let
Such angry passions rise;
Your little hands were never made
To tear each other's eyes.
ISAAC WATTS

A thing moderately good is not so good as it ought to be.
Moderation in temper is always a virtue; but moderation in
principle is always a vice.

—THOMAS PAINE

Struggle diligently against your impatience, and strive to be
amiable and gentle, in season and out of season, towards every one,
however much they may vex and annoy you, and be sure God will
bless your efforts.

—ST. FRANCIS DE SALES

August 2

Trust in him at all times, O people; pour out
your hearts to him, for God is our refuge.
PSALMS 62:8

A mighty fortress is our God,
A bulwark never failing.
Our helper He amid the flood
Of mortal ills prevailing.

MARTIN LUTHER

Go on in all simplicity; do not be so anxious to win a quiet mind, and it will be all the quieter. Do not examine so closely into the progress of your soul. Do not crave so much to be perfect, but let your spiritual life be formed by your duties, and by the actions which are called forth by circumstances. Do not take overmuch thought for to-morrow. God, who has led you Safely on so far, will lead you on to the end. Be altogether at rest in the loving holy confidence which you ought to have in His heavenly Providence.

—ST. FRANCIS DE SALES

August 3

Surely you have granted him eternal blessings
and made him glad with the joy of your presence.

PSALMS 21:6

In the end
these things matter most:
How well did you love?
How fully did you live?
How deeply did you let go.

SIDDHARTHA GAUTAMA

A new day rose upon me. It was as if another sun had risen into the sky; the heavens were indescribably brighter, and the earth fairer; and that day has gone on brightening to the present hour. I have known the other joys of life, I suppose, as much as most men; I have known art and beauty, music and gladness; I have known friendship and love and family ties; but it is certain that till we see GOD in the world—GOD in the bright and boundless universe— we never know the highest joy. It is far more than if one were translated to a world a thousand times fairer than this;for that supreme and central Light of Infinite Love and Wisdom, shining over this world and all worlds, alone can show us how noble and beautiful, how fair and glorious they are.

—ORVILLE DEWEY

August 4

Come, all you who are thirsty,
come to the waters . . . Listen,
listen to me, and eat what is good,
and your soul will delight in the richest of fare . . .
come to me; hear me, that your soul may live.
ISAIAH 55:1-3

Hunger and thirst, O Christ, for sight of thee
Came between me and all the feasts of earth.
Give thou Thyself the Bread, thyself the Wine,
Thou, sole provision for the unknown way.
Long hunger wasted the world wanderer,
With sight of thee may he be satisfied.
RADBOD, BISHOP OF UTRECHT

Gratitude unlocks the fullness of life. It turns what we have into enough, and more. It turns denial into acceptance, chaos to order, confusion to clarity. It can turn a meal into a feast, a house into a home, a stranger into a friend. Gratitude makes sense of our past, brings peace for today and creates a vision for tomorrow.

—MELODY BEATTIE

August 5

Thanks be to God for his indescribable gift!
2 CORINTHIANS 9:15

Every good and perfect gift is from above, coming down from the Father of the heavenly lights . . .
JAMES 1:17

We can give to people who will give us gifts in return. But we're more blessed when we choose to give to those who cannot pay us back.

—JOYCE MEYER

Acknowledging the good that you already have in your life is the foundation for all abundance.

—ECKHART TOLLE

August 6

Praise the Lord,
O my soul, and forget not all his benefits—
PSALMS 103:2

Sweet is the breath of vernal shower,
The bee's collected treasures sweet,
Sweet music's melting fall, but sweeter yet
The still small voice of gratitude.
THOMAS GRAY

Into all our lives, in many simple, familiar, homely ways, God infuses this element of joy from the surprises of life, which unexpectedly brighten our days, and fill our eyes with light. He drops this added sweetness into his children's cup, and makes it to run over. The success we were not counting on, the blessing we were not trying after, the strain of music in the midst of drudgery, the beautiful morning picture or sunset glory thrown in as we pass to or from our daily business, the unsought word of encouragement or expression of sympathy, the sentence that meant for us more than the writer or speaker thought—these and a hundred others that every one's experience can supply are instances of what I mean. You may call it accident or chance—it often is; you may call it human goodness—it often is; but always, always call it God's love for that is always in it. These are the overflowing riches of His grace, these are His free gifts.

—S. LONGFELLOW

Nothing will be impossible for you.
MATTHEW 17:20

So nigh is grandeur to our dust,
So near is God to man,
When Duty whispers low, Thou must,
The youth replies, I can.
RALPH WALDO EMERSON

Now that "Impossible," where truth and mercy and the everlasting
voice of nature order, has no place in the brave man's dictionary.
That when all men have said "Impossible," and tumbled noisily
else whither, and thou alone art left, then first thy time and
possibility have come. It is for thee now: do thou that, and ask
no man's counsel, but thy own only and God's. Brother, thou
hast possibility in thee for much: the possibility of writing on the
eternal skies the record of a heroic life.

—THOMAS CARLYLE

August 8

He whose walk is blameless and who does what is righteous, who speaks the truth from his heart and has no slander on his tongue, who does his neighbor no wrong and casts no slur on his fellowman. . . . He who does these things will never be shaken.

PSALMS 15:2-5

They are slaves who fear to speak
For the fallen and the weak;
They are slaves who will not choose
Hatred, scoffing, and abuse,
Rather than in silence shrink
From the truth they needs must think;
They are slaves who dare not be
In the right with two or three.

J. R. LOWELL

The real corrupters of society may be, not the corrupt, but those who have held back the righteous leaven, the salt that has lost its savor, the innocent who have not even the moral courage to show what they think of the effrontery of impurity—the serious, who yet timidly succumb before some loud-voiced scoffer—the heart trembling all over with religious sensibilities that yet suffers itself through false shame to be beaten down into outward and practical acquiescence by some rude and worldly nature.

—J. H. THOM

First seek the counsel of the Lord.
1 KINGS 22:5

I've many a cross to take up now,
And many left behind;
But present troubles move me not,
Nor shake my quiet mind.
And what may be to-morrow's cross
I never seek to find;
My Father says, "Leave that to me,
And keep a quiet mind."
ANONYMOUS

The mind never puts forth greater power over itself than when, in great trials, it yields up calmly its desires, affections, interests to God. There are seasons when to be still demands immeasurably higher strength than to act. Composure is often the highest result of power. Think you it demands no power to calm the stormy elements of passion, to moderate the vehemence of desire, to throw off the load of dejection, to suppress every repining thought, when the dearest hopes are withered, and to turn the wounded spirit from dangerous reveries and wasting grief, to the quiet discharge of ordinary duties? Is there no power put forth, when a man, stripped of his property, of the fruits of a life's labors, quells discontent and gloomy forebodings, and serenely and patiently returns to the tasks which Providence assigns?

—WILLIAM E. CHANNING

August 10

I have told you these things, so that in me you may have peace.
In this world you will have trouble.
But take heart! I have overcome the world.

JOHN 16:33

WE shall overcome, we shall overcome,
We shall overcome some day
Oh, deep in my heart I do believe
We shall overcome some day.

ANONYMOUS, ADAPTED BY C. ALBERT TINDLEY

The human spirit is as expansive as the cosmos. This is why it is so tragic to belittle yourself or to question your worth. No matter what happens, continue to push back the boundaries of your inner life. The confidence to prevail over any problem, the strength to overcome adversity and unbounded hope — all reside within you.

—DAISAKU IKEDA

August 11

*. . . the Lord your God will bless you in all your work and in
everything you put your hand to.*
DEUTERONOMY 15:10

*God give me work
Till my life shall end
And life
Till my work is done.*
ON THE GRAVE OF WINIFRED HOLTBY

I think I find most help in trying to look on all interruptions
and hindrances to work that one has planned out for oneself as
discipline, trials sent by God to help one against getting selfish
over one's work. Then one can feel that perhaps one's true work—
one's work for God—consists in doing some trifling haphazard
thing that has been thrown into one's day. It is not waste of time,
as one is tempted to think, it is the most important part of the
work of the day—the part one can best offer to God. After such a
hindrance, do not rush after the planned work; trust that the time
to finish it will be given sometime, and keep a quiet heart about it.

—ANNIE KEARY

August 12

*Anyone who does not love remains in death.
Anyone who hates his brother is a murderer, and you know
that no murderer has eternal life in him.*
1 JOHN 3:14-15

What shall I do to gain eternal life?
Discharge aright
The simple dues with which each day is rife
Yea, with thy might.

F. VON SCHILLER

It is no great matter to associate with the good and gentle, for this is naturally pleasing to all, and every one willingly enjoyeth peace, and loveth those best that agree with him. But to be able to live peaceably with hard and perverse persons, or with the disorderly, or with such as go contrary to us, is a great grace, and a most commendable and manly thing.

—ST. THOMAS A. KEMPIS

August 13

"Do it again," he said, and they did it again. "Do it a third time,"
he ordered, and they did it the third time.

1 KINGS 18:34

What though thy way be dark, and earth
With ceaseless care do cark, till mirth
To thee no sweet strain singeth;
Still hide thy life above, and still
Believe that God is love; fulfil
Whatever lot He bringeth.

ALBERT E. EVANS

Have courage for the great sorrows of life and patience for the small ones; and when you have laboriously accomplished your daily task, go to sleep in peace. God is awake.

—VICTOR HUGO

August 14

. . . by the power of God, who has saved us and called us to a holy life—not because of anything we have done but because of his own purpose and grace.
TIMOTHY 1:8-9

Amazing grace! How sweet the sound
That saved a wretch like me!
I once was lost, but now am found,
Was blind, but now I see.
JOHN NEWTON

Religion in its humility restores man to his only dignity, the courage to live by grace.

—GEORGE SANTAYANA

Will is to grace as the horse is to the rider.

—ST. AUGUSTINE

For God did not give us a spirit of timidity, but a spirit of power,
of love and of self-discipline.
2 TIMOTHY 1:7

Therefore, prepare your minds for action; be self-controlled . . .
1 PETER 1:13

Here's one of my favorite statements: We are never going to enjoy
stability, we are never going to enjoy spiritual maturity until we
learn how to do what's right when it feels wrong, and every time
you do what's right by a decision of your will using discipline and
self control to go beyond how you feel, the more painful it is in
your flesh, the more you're growing spiritually at that particular
moment.

—JOYCE MEYER

Happiness comes from righteous living and the development of a
noble character. You can observe this by noticing that people who
are truly happy are honest, unselfish, kind, responsible and have
a high moral standards. On the other hand, unhappy people are
invariably selfish, lazy, irresponsible and lacking of self discipline.
And people who are miserable tend to be immoral, dishonest,
greedy, cruel, or in other ways dark in character.

—HELEN B. ANDELIN

. . . those who plow evil and those who sow trouble reap it.
JOB 4:8

The life above, when this is past,
Is the ripe fruit of life below.
Sow love, and taste its fruitage pure;
Sow peace, and reap its harvest bright
Sow sunbeams on the rock and moor,
And find a harvest-home of light.
H. BONAR

If you send out goodness from yourself, or if you share that
which is happy or good within you, it will all come back to you
multiplied ten thousand times. In the kingdom of love there is no
competition; there is no possessiveness or control. The more love
you give away, the more love you will have.

—JOHN O'DONOHUE

August 17

Turn to me and have mercy on me . . .
PSALMS 86:16

No ceremony that to great ones longs,
Not the king's crown, nor the deputed sword,
The marshal's truncheon, nor the judge's robe,
Become them with one half so good a grace
As mercy does.
WILLIAM SHAKESPEARE

Be like the sun for grace and mercy. Be like the night to cover others' faults. Be like running water for generosity. Be like death for rage and anger. Be like the Earth for modesty. Appear as you are. Be as you appear.

—RUMI

August 18

The fruits of righteousness will be peace; the effect of righteousness will be quietness and confidence forever.
ISAIAH 32:17

I learned this, at least, by my experiment: that if one advances
confidently in the direction of his dreams, and endeavors to live
the life which he has imagined, he will meet with a success
unexpected in common hours.
HENRY DAVID THOREAU

Nothing doth so much establish the mind amidst the rollings
and turbulency of present things, as both a look above them, and
a look beyond them; above them to the good and steady Hand by
which they are ruled, and beyond them to the sweet and beautiful
end to which, by that Hand, they shall be brought. . . . Study pure
and holy walking, if you would have your confidence firm, and
have boldness and joy in God. You will find that a little sin will
shake your trust and disturb your peace more than the greatest
sufferings: yea, in those sufferings, your assurance and joy in God
will grow and abound most if sin be kept out. So much sin as gets
in, so much peace will go out.

—R. LEIGHTON

August 19

I will lead them beside streams of water on a level path where they will
not stumble, because I am Israel's father . . .
JEREMIAH 31:9

Lead, kindly Light, amid the encircling gloom;
Lead Thou me on!
The night is dark, and I am far from home,
Lead Thou me on!
Keep Thou my feet; I do not ask to see
The distant scene; one step enough for me.
JOHN HENRY CARDINAL NEWMAN

Far away there in the sunshine are my highest aspirations. I may not reach them, but I can look up and see their beauty, believe in them, and try to follow where they lead.

—LOUISA MAY ALCOTT

To bring things about for yourself, taking all He sends joyfully, and believing the "one step" set before you to be enough for you.

—JEAN NICOLAS GROU

August 20

It is God who arms me with strength and makes my way perfect.
PSALMS 18:32

My strength is as the strength of ten,
Because my heart is pure.
LORD ALFRED TENNYSON

We require a certain firmness in all circumstances of life, even the happiest, and perhaps contradictions come in order to prove and exercise this; and, if we can only determine so to use them, the very effort brings back tranquility to the soul, which always enjoys having exercised its strength in conformity to duty.

—WILLIAM VON HUMBOLDT

August 21

For none of us lives to himself alone and none of us dies to himself alone.
ROMANS 14:7

If there be some weaker one,
Give me strength to help him on;
If a blinder soul there be,
Let me guide him nearer Thee.
J. G. WHITTIER

No man is an island, entire of itself; every man is a piece of the continent, a part of the main; if a clod be washed away by the sea, Europe is the less, as well as if a promontory were, as well as if a manor of thy friends or of thine own were; any man's death diminishes me, because I am involved in mankind; and therefore never send to know for whom the bell tolls; it tolls for thee.

—JOHN DONNE

Try to put yourself in another's place . . . Cultivate the habit of sympathy.

—G.H. WILKINSON

August 22

What is impossible with men is possible with God.
LUKE 18:27

High hearts are never long without hearing some new call, some distant clarion of God, even in their dreams; and soon they are observed to break up the camp of ease, and start on some fresh march of faithful service. And, looking higher still, we find those who never wait till their moral work accumulates, and who reward resolution with no rest; with whom, therefore, the alternation is instantaneous and constant; who do the good only to see the better, and see the better only to achieve it; who are too meek for transport, too faithful for remorse, too earnest for repose; whose worship is action and whose action ceaseless aspiration.

—J. MARTINEAU

August 23

. . . nor is it honorable to seek one's own honor.
PROVERBS 25:27

Should you then seek great things for yourself? Seek them not.
JEREMIAH 45:5

My crown is in my heart, not on my head;
Not deck'd with diamonds and Indian stones,
Nor to be seen: my crown is call'd content;
A crown it is that seldom kings enjoy.
WILLIAM SHAKESPEARE

I am not sure exactly what heaven will be like, but I know that when we die and it comes time for God to judge us, he will not ask, "How many good things have you done in your life?" rather he will ask, "How much love did you put into what you did?".

—MOTHER TERESA

August 24

. . . it is easier for a camel to go through the eye of a needle than for a rich man to enter the kingdom of God.
MATTHEW 19:24

Preserve me from my calling's snare,
And hide my simple heart above,
Above the thorns of choking care,
The gilded baits of worldly love.
C. WESLEY

We must rapidly begin the shift from a "thing-oriented" society to a "person-oriented" society. When machines and computers, profit motives and property rights are considered more important than people, the giant triplets of racism, materialism, and militarism are incapable of being conquered.

—MARTIN LUTHER KING, JR.

August 25

See to it that you do not refuse him who speaks.
HEBREWS 12:25

We do not believe in ourselves until someone reveals that deep inside us something is valuable, worth listening to, worthy of our trust, sacred to our touch. Once we believe in ourselves we can risk curiosity, wonder, spontaneous delight or any experience that reveals the human spirit.
E.E. CUMMINGS

I have faith that God will show you the answer. But you have to understand that sometimes it takes a while to be able to recognize what God wants you to do. That's how it often is. God's voice is usually nothing more than a whisper, and you have to listen very carefully to hear it. But other times, in those rarest of moments, the answer is obvious and rings as loud as a church bell.

—NICHOLAS SPARKS

August 26

Do not be quick with your mouth, do not be hasty in your heart to utter anything before God.

ECCLESIASTES 5:2

Be still before the Lord . . .

ZECHARIAH 2:13

From the world of sin and noise
And hurry I withdraw;
For the small and inward voice
I wait with humble awe
Silent am I now and still,
Dare not in Thy presence move;
To my waiting soul reveal
The secret of Thy love.

C. WESLEY

It is only with the pious affection of the will that we can be spiritually attentive to God. As long as the noisy restlessness of the thoughts goes on, the gentle and holy desires of the new nature are overpowered and inactive.

—J. P. GREAVES

There is hardly ever a complete silence in our soul. God is whispering to us wellnigh incessantly. Whenever the sounds of the world die out in the soul, or sink low, then we hear these whisperings of God. He is always whispering to us, only we do not always hear, because of the noise, hurry, and distraction which life causes as it rushes on.

—F. W. FABER

August 27

. . . he who stands firm to the end will be saved.
MATTHEW 10:22

Teach me, O God, so to use all the circumstances of my life today that they may bring forth in me the fruits of holiness rather than the fruits of sin.

Let me use disappointments as material for patience:
Let me use success as material for thankfulness:
Let me use suspense as material for perseverance:
Let me use danger as material for courage:
Let me use reproach as material for longsuffering:
Let me use praise as material for humility:
Let me use pleasure as material for temperance:
Let me use pains as material for endurance.
JOHN BAILLIE

Perserverence is a great element of success. If you only knock
long enough and loud enough at the gate, you are sure to wake up
somebody.

—HENRY WADSWORTH LONGFELLOW

August 28

*Yet this I call to mind and therefore I have hope: Because of the
Lord's great love we are not consumed, for his compassions never fail.*
LAMENTATIONS 3:21-22

*Because I could not stop for Death –
He kindly stopped for me –
The Carriage held but just Ourselves –
And Immortality.*
EMILY DICKINSON

He is immortal, not because he alone among creatures has an
inexhaustible voice, but because he has a soul, a spirit capable of
compassion and sacrifice and endurance.

—WILLIAM FAULKNER

August 29

If anyone says, "I love God," yet hates his brother, he is a liar.
JOHN 5:20

Because I held upon my selfish road,
And left my brother wounded by the way,
And called ambition duty, and pressed on—
Lord, I do repent.
SARAH WILLIAMS

Try to understand men. If you understand each other you will be kind to each other. Knowing a man well never leads to hate and almost always leads to love.

—JOHN STEINBECK

August 30

. . . I urge you to live a life worthy of the calling you have received.
Be completely humble and gentle;
be patient, bearing with one another in love.
EPHESIANS 4:1-2

Give us grace and strength to forbear and to persevere . . . Give us courage and gaiety and the quiet mind, spare to us our friends, soften to us our enemies.

—ROBERT LOUIS STEVENSON

How many are the sufferers who have fallen amongst misfortunes along the wayside of life! By chance, we come that way; chance, accident, Providence, has thrown them in our way; we see them from a distance, like the Priest, or we come upon them suddenly, like the Levite; our business, our pleasure, is interrupted by the sight, is troubled by the delay; what are our feelings, what our actions towards them? . . . "Who is thy neighbor?" It is the sufferer, wherever, whoever, whatsoever he be. Wherever thou hearest the cry of distress, wherever thou seest any one brought across thy path by the chances and changes of life (that is, by the Providence of God), whom it is in thy power to help—he, stranger or enemy though he be—he is thy neighbor.

—A.P. STANLEY

August 31

He was oppressed and afflicted, yet he did not open his mouth.
ISAIAH 53:7

Go, bury thy sorrow,
The world hath its share
Go, bury it deeply,
Go, hide it with care
Go, bury thy sorrow,
Let others be blest
Go, give them the sunshine,
And tell God the rest.
ANONYMOUS

The belief that unhappiness is selfless and happiness is selfish
is misguided. It's more selfless to act happy. It takes energy,
generosity, and discipline to be unfailingly lighthearted, yet
everyone takes the happy person for granted. No one is careful
of his feelings or tries to keep his spirits high. He seems self-
sufficient; he becomes a cushion for others. And because happiness
seems unforced, that person usually gets no credit.

—GRETCHEN RUBIN

Strive to realize a state of inward happiness,
independent of circumstances.

—J. P. GREAVES

September

September 1

As a mother comforts her child,
so will I comfort you . . .

ISAIAH 66:13

Rejoice with Jerusalem and be glad for her,
all you who love her;
rejoice greatly with her,
all you who mourn over her.
For you will nurse and be satisfied
at her comforting breasts;
you will drink deeply
and delight in her overflowing abundance . . .
I will extend peace to her like a river,
and the wealth of nations like a flooding stream;
you will nurse and be carried on her arm
and dandled on her knees.

ISAIAH 66:10-12

II hear my father; I need never fear.
I hear my mother; I shall never be lonely, or want for love.
When I am hungry it is they who provide for me; when I am in
dismay, it is they who fill me with comfort.
When I am astonished or bewildered, it is they who make the weak
ground firm beneath my soul: it is in them that I put my trust.
When I am sick it is they who send for the doctor; when I am well
and happy, it is in their eyes that I know best that I am loved; and
it is towards the shining of their smiles that I lift up my heart and
in their laughter that I know my best delight.

I hear my father and my mother and they are my giants, my king
and my queen, beside whom there are not others so wise or worthy
or honorable or brave or beautiful in this world.
I need never fear: nor ever shall I lack for loving-kindness.

—JAMES AGEE

I have calmed and quieted my soul, like a child quieted at its
mother's breast: like a child that is quieted is my soul.

—ANONYMOUS
(BASED ON PSALMS 131:3)

September 2

If it is possible, as far as it depends on you,
live at peace with everyone.
ROMANS 12:18

O God of many names
Lover of all nations
We pray for peace
in our hearts
in our homes
in our nations
in our world
The peace of your will
The peace of your need.
GEORGE APPLETON

Have you ever thought seriously of the meaning of that blessing given to the peacemakers? People are always expecting to get peace in heaven; but you know whatever peace they get there will be ready-made. Whatever making of peace they can be blest for, must be on the earth here: not the taking of arms against, but the building of nests amidst, its 'sea of troubles' like the halcyons. Difficult enough, you think? Perhaps so, but I do not see that any of us try. We complain of the want of many things—we want votes, we want liberty, we want amusement, we want money. Which of us feels or knows that he wants peace?

—JOHN RUSKIN

September 3

Whoever loves discipline loves knowledge,
but he who hates correction is stupid.
PROVERBS 12:1

Why do they always teach us that it's easy and evil to do what we want and that we need discipline to restrain ourselves? It's the hardest thing in the world—to do what we want. And it takes the greatest kind of courage. I mean, what we really want.

—AYN RAND

But his delight is in the law of the Lord . . .
He is like a tree planted by streams of water,
which yields its fruit in season and whose leaf does not wither.
Whatever he does prospers.

PSALMS1:2-3

I have learned
To look on nature, not as in the hour
Of thoughtless youth; but hearing oftentimes
The still, sad music of humanity,
Nor harsh nor grating, though of ample power
To chasten and subdue. And I have felt
A presence that disturbs me with the joy
Of elevated thoughts; a sense sublime
Of something far more deeply interfused,
Whose dwelling is the light of setting suns,
And the round ocean and the living air,
And the blue sky, and in the mind of man:
A motion and a spirit, that impels
All thinking things, all objects of all thought,
And rolls through all things.

WILLIAM WORDSWORTH

Our task must be to free ourselves. . . by widening our circle of
compassion to embrace all living creatures and the whole of nature
and it's beauty.

—ALBERT EINSTEIN

September 5

Come unto me, all you who are weary and burdened,
and I will give you rest.
Take my yoke upon you and learn from me,
for I am gentle and humble in heart,
and you will find rest for your souls.
MATTHEW 11:28-29

Blessed mood,
In which the burthen of the mystery,
In which the heavy and the weary weight
Of all this unintelligible world,
Is lightened.
WILLIAM WORDSWORTH

Any task in life is easier if we approach it with the one at a time attitude. ... To cite a whimsical saying; "If you chase two rabbits, both of them will escape.'" No one is adequate to do everything all at once. We have to select what is important, what is possible, and begin where we are, with what we have. And if we begin and if we keep going the weight, the worry, the doubt, the depression will begin to lift. . . .We can't do everything always, but we can do something now, and doing something will help to lift the weight and lessen the worry, "The beginning," said Plato, "is the most important part."

—RICHARD L. EVANS

Test me, O Lord, and try me,
examine my heart and my mind . . .
PSALMS 26:2

Sometimes the greatest tests of our strength are situations that
don't seem so obviously dangerous. Sometimes surviving is the
hardest thing of all.
RICHELLE MEAD

If you're going to try, go all the way. Otherwise, don't even start.
This could mean losing girlfriends, wives, relatives and maybe even
your mind. It could mean not eating for three or four days. It could
mean freezing on a park bench. It could mean jail. It could mean
derision. It could mean mockery—isolation. Isolation is the gift.
All the others are a test of your endurance, of how much you really
want to do it. And, you'll do it, despite rejection and the worst
odds. And it will be better than anything else you can imagine.
If you're going to try, go all the way. There is no other feeling like
that. You will be alone with the gods, and the nights will flame
with fire. You will ride life straight to perfect laughter. It's the only
good fight there is.

—CHARLES BUKOWSKI

September 7

For the Lord comforts his people
and will have compassion on his afflicted ones.
ISAIAH 49:13

Religion that God our Father accepts
as pure and faultless is this:
to look after orphans and widows in their distress . . .
JAMES 1:27

Awake, my charity, and feed
The hungry soul, and clothe the poor;
In heaven are found no sons of need,
There all these duties are no more.
ANONYMOUS

For attractive lips, speak words of kindness.
For lovely eyes, seek out the good in people.
For a slim figure, share your food with the hungry.
For beautiful hair, let a child run their fingers through it once a day.
For poise, walk with the knowledge that you never walk alone.
People, more than things, have to be restored, renewed, revived, reclaimed, and redeemed. Remember, if you ever need a helping hand, you will find one at the end of each of your arms.
As you grow older, you will discover that you have two hands, one for helping yourself and the other for helping others.

—SAM LEVENSON

Be on your guard; stand firm in the faith;
be men of courage; be strong.
1 CORINTHIANS 16:13

So you plant your garden and decorate your own soul,
Instead of waiting for someone to bring you flowers.
And you learn that you really can endure. . .
That you really are strong
And you really do have worth. . .
And you learn and learn. . .
With every good-bye you learn.
JORGE LUIS BORGES

Therefore, dear Sir, love your solitude and try to sing out with the pain it causes you. For those who are near you are far away... and this shows that the space around you is beginning to grow vast.... be happy about your growth, in which of course you can't take anyone with you, and be gentle with those who stay behind; be confident and calm in front of them and don't torment them with your doubts and don't frighten them with your faith or joy, which they wouldn't be able to comprehend. Seek out some simple and true feeling of what you have in common with them, which doesn't necessarily have to alter when you yourself change again and again; when you see them, love life in a form that is not your own and be indulgent toward those who are growing old, who are afraid of the aloneness that you trust.... and don't expect any understanding; but believe in a love that is being stored up for you like an inheritance, and have faith that in this love there is a strength and a blessing so large that you can travel as far as you wish without having to step outside it.

—RAINER MARIA RILKE

September 9

This is a trustworthy saying. And I want you to stress these things, so that those who have trusted in God may be careful to devote themselves to doing what is good.
TITUS 3:8

Whate'er is noble, pure, refined,
Just, generous, amiable, and kind,
That may my constant thoughts pursue,
That may I love and practice too.
ANONYMOUS

One secret act of self-denial, one sacrifice of inclination to duty, is worth all the mere good thoughts, warm feelings, passionate prayers, in which idle people indulge themselves.

—J. H. NEWMAN

Our prime purpose in this life is to help others. And if you can't help them, at least don't hurt them.

—DALAI LAMA XIV

Do you not know that your body is a temple of the Holy Spirit,
who is in you, whom you have received from God?. . .
Therefore honor God with your body.
CORINTHIANS 6:19-20

Here, Lord, before you tonight are the bodies of sleeping men:
The pure body of the tiny child,
The soiled body of the prostitute,
The vigorous body of the athlete,
The exhausted body of the factory worker,
The soft body of the playboy,
The surfeited body of the poor man,
The paralyzed body of the cripple,
All bodies, Lord, of all ages.

I offer them all to you, Lord, and ask you to bless them,
. . . May these bodies be developed, purified, transfigured,
By those who dwell in them.
MICHEL QUOIST

The human body is an instrument for the production of art in the life of the human soul.

—ALFRED NORTH WHITEHEAD

This is what you shall do; Love the earth and sun and the animals, despise riches, give alms to every one that asks, stand up for the stupid and crazy, devote your income and labor to others, hate tyrants, argue not concerning God, have patience and indulgence toward the people, take off your hat to nothing known or unknown or to any man or number of men, go freely with powerful uneducated persons and with the young and with the mothers of families, read these leaves in the open air every season of every year of your life, re-examine all you have been told at school or church or in any book, dismiss whatever insults your own soul, and your very flesh shall be a great poem and have the richest fluency not only in its words but in the silent lines of its lips and face and between the lashes of your eyes and in every motion and joint of your body.

—WALT WHITMAN

September 11

. . . your kingdom come,
your will be done on earth as it is in heaven.
MATTHEW 6:10

To do his heavenly Father's will
Was his employment and delight;
Humility and holy zeal
Shone through his life divinely bright.
ANONYMOUS

I've come to believe that each of us has a personal calling that's as unique as a fingerprint—and that the best way to succeed is to discover what you love and then find a way to offer it to others in the form of service, working hard, and also allowing the energy of the universe to lead you.

—OPRAH WINFREY

If you do not wish for His kingdom, don't pray for it. But if you do, you must do more than pray for it; you must work for it.

—JOHN RUSKIN

She obeys no one, she accepts no correction.
She does not trust in the Lord,
she does not draw near to her God.
ZEPHANIAH 3:2

To avoid criticism say nothing,
do nothing, be nothing.
ARISTOTLE

It is not the critic who counts; not the man who points out how the strong man stumbles, or where the doer of deeds could have done them better. The credit belongs to the man who is actually in the arena, whose face is marred by dust and sweat and blood; who strives valiantly; who errs, who comes short again and again, because there is no effort without error and shortcoming; but who does actually strive to do the deeds; who knows great enthusiasms, the great devotions; who spends himself in a worthy cause; who at the best knows in the end the triumph of high achievement, and who at the worst, if he fails, at least fails while daring greatly, so that his place shall never be with those cold and timid souls who neither know victory nor defeat.

—THEODORE ROOSEVELT

September 13

Brothers, if someone is caught in a sin, you who are spiritual should restore him gently. But watch yourself, or you also may be tempted. Carry each other's burdens, and in this way you will fulfill the law of Christ.
GALATIANS 6:1-2

When another person makes you suffer, it is because he suffers deeply within himself, and his suffering is spilling over. He does not need punishment; he needs help. That's the message he is sending.
THICH NHAT HANH

The Bible says, "If you walk with wise men, then you're going to become wise." If you associate with successful people, before long you will become successful. Their enthusiasm will be contagious and you will catch that vision. If you stay in an atmosphere of victory, before long you're going to have an image of victory. If you hang around people of faith, before long you're going to be filled with faith. But you cannot soar with the eagles as long as you're pecking around with the chickens.

—JOEL OSTEEN

Call to me and I will answer you and tell you great and unsearchable things you do not know.

JEREMIAH 33:3

Prayer is the soul's sincere desire,
Uttered or unexpressed;
The motion of a hidden fire
That trembles in the breast.

JAMES MONTGOMERY

If you have any trial which seems intolerable, pray—pray and it be relieved or changed. There is no harm in that. We may pray for anything, not wrong in itself, with perfect freedom, if we do not pray selfishly. One disabled from duty by sickness may pray for health, that he may do his work; or one hemmed in by internal impediments may pray for utterance, that he may serve better the truth and the right. Or, if we have a besetting sin, we may pray to be delivered from it, in order to serve God and man, and not be ourselves Satans to mislead and destroy. But the answer to the prayer may be, as it was to Paul, not the removal of the thorn, but, instead, a growing insight into its meaning and value. The voice of God in our soul may show us, as we look up to Him, that His strength is enough to enable us to bear it.

—J. F. CLARKE

September 15

Brothers, as an example of patience in the face of suffering, take the prophets who spoke in the name of the Lord. As you know, we consider blessed those who have persevered. You have heard of Job's perseverance and have seen what the Lord finally brought about.

JAMES 5:10-11

Simplicity, patience, compassion.
These three are your greatest treasures.
Simple in actions and thoughts, you return to the source of being.
Patient with both friends and enemies,
you accord with the way things are.
Compassionate toward yourself,
you reconcile all beings in the world.

LAO TZU

A waiting person is a patient person. The word patience means the willingness to stay where we are and live the situation out to the full in the belief that something hidden there will manifest itself to us.

—HENRI J.M. NOUWEN

September 16

I tell you the truth, if you have faith as small as a mustard seed, you can say to this mountain, "Move from here to there" and it will move. Nothing will be impossible for you."

MATTHEW 17:20

We find great things are made of little things,
And little things go lessening till at last
Comes God behind them.
ROBERT BROWNING

John Lennon once said, "Life is what happens when you're busy making other plans." For me, life is what was happening while I was busy waiting for my big moment. I was ready for it and believed that the rest of my life would fade into the background, and that my big moment would carry me through life like a lifeboat. The Big Moment, unfortunately, is an urban myth. Some people have them, in a sense, when they win the Heisman or become the next American Idol. But even that football player or that singer is living a life made up of more than that one moment. Life is a collection of a million, billion moments, tiny little moments and choices, like a handful of luminous, glowing pearl. It takes so much time, and so much work, and those beads and moments are so small, and so much less fabulous and dramatic than the movies. But this is what I'm finding, in glimpses and flashes: this is it. This is it, in the best possible way. That thing I'm waiting for, that adventure, that move-score-worthy experience unfolding gracefully. This is it. Normal, daily life ticking by on our streets and sidewalks, in our houses and apartments, in our beds and at our dinner tables, in our dreams and prayers and fights and secrets —this pedestrian life is the most precious thing any of use will ever experience.

—SHAUNA NIEQUIST

September 17

. . . whoever wants to become great among you must be your servant,
and whoever wants to be first must be slave of all.
MATTHEW 10:43

All service ranks the same with God:
With God, whose puppets, best and worst,
Are we, there is no last or first.
ROBERT BROWNING

Everybody can be great...because anybody can serve. You don't
have to have a college degree to serve. You don't have to make your
subject and verb agree to serve. You only need a heart full of grace.
A soul generated by love.

—MARTIN LUTHER KING, JR.

September 18

All the ways of the Lord are loving and faithful
for those who keep the demands of his covenant.
PSALMS 25:10

In peace, Love tunes the shepherd's reed;
In war, he mounts the warrior's steed;
In halls, in gay attire is seen;
In hamlets, dances on the green.
Love rules the court, the camp, the grove,
And men below, and saints above;
For love is heaven, and heaven is love.

SIR WALTER SCOTT

To recognize with delight all high and generous and beautiful actions; to find a joy even in seeing the good qualities of your bitterest opponents, and to admire those qualities even in those with whom you have least sympathy, be it either the Romanist or the Unitarian, this is the only spirit which can heal the love of slander and of calumny.

—F. W. ROBERTSON

September 19

Pray that the Lord your God will tell us where
we should go and what we should do.

JEREMIAH 42:3

The best way to find yourself is to lose yourself
in the service of others.

MAHATMA GANDHI

We can't choose happiness either for ourselves or for another; we can't tell where that will lie. We can only choose whether we will indulge ourselves in the present moment, or whether we will renounce that, for the sake of obeying the Divine voice within us,—for the sake of being true to all the motives that sanctify our lives. I know this belief is hard; it has slipped away from me again and again; but I have felt that if I let it go forever, I should have no light through the darkness of this life.

—GEORGE ELIOT

September 20

Rescue me from my enemies, O Lord, for I hide myself in you.

PSALMS 143:9

The best way to destroy an enemy is to make him a friend.
ABRAHAM LINCOLN

I have known the joy and pain of friendship. I have served and been served. I have made some good enemies for which I am not a bit sorry. I have loved unselfishly, and I have fondled hatred with the red-hot tongs of Hell. That's living.

—ZORA NEALE HURSTON

I long to dwell in your tent forever and
take refuge in the shelter of your wings.

PSALMS 61:4

> *He drew a circle that shut me out-*
> *Heretic , rebel, a thing to flout.*
> *But love and I had the wit to win:*
> *We drew a circle and took him In!*

ANONYMOUS

Like an ant on a stick both ends of which are burning, I go to
and fro without knowing what to do and in great despair. Like
the inescapable shadow which follows me, the dead weight of sin
haunts me. Graciously look upon me. Thy love is my refuge.

—EDWIN MARKHAM

The grass withers and the flowers fall,
but the word of God stands forever.
ISAIAH 40:8

Bless'd are the souls that hear and know
The gospel's joyful sound;
Peace shall attend the path they go,
And light their steps surround.
ANONYMOUS

The gospel is like a fresh, mild, and cool air in the extreme heat of summer, a solace and comfort in the anguish of the conscience. But as this heat proceeds from the rays of the sun, so likewise the terrifying of the conscience must proceed from the preaching of the law, to the end that we may know we have offended against the laws of God.

—MARTIN LUTHER

Show me your ways, O lord, teach me your paths;
guide me in your truth and teach me. . .
PSALMS 25:4-5

Tell me and I forget,
teach me and I may remember,
involve me and I learn.
ERIC MILNER-WHITE

There is nothing like the first glance we get at duty, before there
has been any special pleading of our affections or inclinations.
Duty is never uncertain at first. It is only after we have got
involved in the mazes and sophistries of wishing that things were
otherwise than they are, that it seems indistinct. Considering a
duty is often only explaining it away. Deliberation is often only
dishonesty. God's guidance is plain, when we are true.

—F. W. ROBERTSON

September 24

. . . . wake up and shout for joy.
ISAIAH 26:19

Perhaps it is better to wake up after all,
even to suffer, rather than to remain
a dupe to illusions all one's life.
KATE CHOPIN

With his first waking consciousness, he can set himself to take a serious, manly view of the day before him. He ought to know pretty well on what lines his difficulty is likely to come, whether in being irritable, or domineering, or sharp in his bargains, or self absorbed, or whatever it be; and now, in this quiet hour, he can take a good, full look at his enemy, and make up his mind to beat him. It is a good time, too, for giving his thoughts a range quite beyond himself—beyond even his own moral struggles—a good time, there in the stillness, for going into the realm of other lives. His wife—what needs has she for help, for sympathy, that he can meet? His children, how can he make the day sweeter to them? This acquaintance, who is having a hard time; this friend, who dropped a word to you yesterday that you hardly noticed in your hurry, but that comes up to you now, revealing in him some finer trait, some deeper hunger, than you had guessed before—now you can think these things over. So you get your day somewhat into right perspective and proportion before you begin it.

—G. S. MERRIAM

September 25

There, in the presence of the Lord your God,
you and your families shall eat and
rejoice in everything you have put your hand to,
because the Lord your God has blessed you.
DEUTERONOMY 12:7

'Mid pleasures and palaces though we may roam,
Be it ever so humble, there's no place like home.
JOHN HOWARD PAYNE

We ought daily or weekly to dedicate a little time to the reckoning up of the virtues of our belongings—wife, children, friends—and contemplating them then in a beautiful collection. And we should do so now, that we may not pardon and love in vain and too late, after the beloved one has been taken away from us to a better world.

—JEAN PAUL RICHTER

September 26

Go and enjoy choice food and sweet drinks, and send some to those who have nothing prepared.
NEHEMIAH 8:10

Enjoy the little things in life, for one day you'll look back and realize they were big things.
KURT VONNEGUT

As the hand is made for holding and the eye for seeing, thou hast fashioned me for joy. Share with me the vision that shall find it everywhere: in the wild violet's beauty; in the lark's melody; in the face of a steadfast man; in a child's smile; in a mother's love; in the purity of Jesus.

—GAELIC PRAYER

September 27

In him was life, and that life was the light of men.
JOHN 1: 4

I would rather walk with a friend in the dark,
than alone in the light.
HELEN KELLER

Suppose you are bewildered and know not what is right nor what is true. Can you not cease to regard whether you do or not, whether you be bewildered, whether you be happy? Cannot you utterly and perfectly love, and rejoice to be in the dark, and gloom-beset, because that very thing is the fact of God's Infinite Being as it is to you? Cannot you take this trial also into your own heart, and be ignorant, not because you are obliged, but because that being God's will, it is yours also? Do you not see that a person who truly loves is one with the Infinite Being—cannot be uncomfortable or unhappy? It is that which is that he wills and desires and holds best of all to be. To know God is utterly to sacrifice self.

—JAMES HINTON

September 28

*Dear children, let us not love with words or
tongue but with actions and in truth.*
I JOHN 3:18

*O Do you want to know who you are?
Don't ask. Act! Action will delineate and define you.*
THOMAS JEFFERSON

Twenty years from now you will be more disappointed by the things that you didn't do than by the ones you did do. So throw off the bowlines. Sail away from the safe harbor. Catch the trade winds in your sails. Explore. Dream. Discover.

—MARK TWAIN

Don't be too timid and squeamish about your actions. All life is an experiment. The more experiments you make the better.

—RALPH WALDO EMERSON

September 29

*"These people come near to me with their mouth
and honor me with their lips, but their hearts are far from me."*
ISAIAH 29:13

Joy to the world! the Lord is come;
Let earth receive her King.
Let ev'ry heart prepare Him room,
And heav'n and nature sing.

ISAAC WATTS

Lord, take my lips and speak through them; take my mind and think through it; take my heart and set it on fire.

—W. H. H. AITKEN

Love doesn't need reason. It speaks from the irrational wisdom of the heart.

—DEEPAK CHOPRA

September 30

The arrogant mock me without restraint, but I do not
turn from your law . . . Your decrees are the theme
of my song wherever I lodge.

PSALMS 119:51-54

He is not strong and powerful who throweth people down;
but he is strong who witholdeth himself from anger.

MUHAMMAD

To hold our tongues when everyone is gossiping, to smile without hostility at people and institutions, to compensate for the shortage of love in the world with more love in small, private matters; to be more faithful in our work, to show greater patience, to forgo the cheap revenge obtainable from mockery and criticism: all these are things we can do.

—HERMANN HESSE

October

Lazy hands make a man poor, but diligent hands bring wealth.
PROVERBS 10:4

> For what is life if measured by the space,
> Not by the act?
> Or masked man, if valued by his face,
> Above his fact?
> Here's one outlived his peers
> And told forth fourscore years:
> He vexed time, and busied the whole state,
> Troubled both foes and friends,
> But ever to no ends:
> What did this stirrer but die late?
> How well at twenty had he fall'n or stood!
> For three of his four score, he did no good.

BEN JOHNSON

To laugh often and love much; to win the respect of intelligent persons and the affection of children; to earn the approbation of honest citizens and endure the betrayal of false friends; to appreciate beauty; to find the best in others; to give of one's self; to leave the world a bit better, whether by a healthy child, a garden patch or a redeemed social condition; to have played and laughed with enthusiasm and sung with exultation; to know even one life has breathed easier because you have lived—this is to have succeeded.

—BESSIE ANDERSON STANLEY

October 2

*My words come from an upright heart;
my lips sincerely speak what I know.*
JOB 33:3

*Great minds discuss ideas.
Average minds discuss events.
Small minds discuss people.*
ELEANOR ROOSEVELT

Do not flatter yourself that your thoughts are under due control, your desires properly regulated, or your dispositions subject as they should be to Christian principle, if your intercourse with others consists mainly of frivolous gossip, impertinent anecdotes, speculations on the character and affairs of your neighbours, the repetition of former conversations, or a discussion of the current petty scandal of society; much less, if you allow yourself in careless exaggeration on all these points, and that grievous inattention to exact truth, which is apt to attend the statements of those whose conversation is made up of these materials.

—H. WARE, JR.

October 3

. . . you who pass judgment on someone else, for at whatever point you judge the other, you are condemning yourself, because you who pass judgment do the same things.

ROMANS 2:1

Judge not; the workings of his brain
And of his heart thou canst not see;
What looks to thy dim eyes a stain,
In God's pure light rnay only be
A scar, brought from some well-won field,
Where thou wouldst only faint and yield.

ADELAIDE A. PROCTER

The world has often seen examples of the presumptuous religious individual who is perfectly secure in his own God-relationship, flippantly assured of his own salvation, but self-importantly engaged in doubting the salvation of others and in offering to help them. However, I believe it would be a fitting expression for a genuinely religious attitude if the individual were to say: "I do not doubt the salvation of any human being; the only one I have fears about is myself. Even when I see a man sink very low, I should never presume to doubt his salvation; but if it were myself, I should doubtless have to suffer this terrible thought." A genuine religious personality is always mild in his judgment of others, and only in his relation to himself is he cold and strict as a master inquisitor. His attitude towards others is like that of a benevolent patriarch

to the younger generation; in relation to himself he is old and
incorruptible.

—SØREN KIERKEGAARD

October 4

"For I know the plans I have for you," declares the Lord,
"Plans to prosper you and not harm you,
plans to give you hope and a future."
JEREMIAH 29:11

Live as if you were to die tomorrow.
Learn as if you were to live forever.
MAHATMA GANDHI

Watch your way then, as a cautious traveler; and don't be gazing
at that mountain or river in the distance, and saying, "How shall
I ever get over them?" but keep to the present little inch that is
before you, and accomplish that in the little moment that belongs
to it. The mountain and the river can only be passed in the same
way; and, when you come to them, you will come to the light and
strength that belong to them.

—M. A. KELTY

Let not future things disturb thee, for thou wilt come to them, if it
shall be necessary, having with thee the same reason which thou
now usest for present things.

—MARCUS ANTONINUS

October 5

They approach and come forward;
each helps the other and says to his brother,
"Be strong!"
ISAIAH 41:5-6

. . . say to those with fearful hearts, "Be strong, do not fear . . . "
ISAIAH 35:4

When weaker Christians we despise,
We do the great Redeemer wrong;
For God, the gracious and the wise,
Receives the feeble with the strong.
ANONYMOUS

I think we often fail by our own foolishness, impulsiveness, or selfishness, and hurt people needlessly (some are called to punish as a duty, that is another matter), and still God may overrule it; yet that will be no excuse for our self-confidence, or rudeness, or hastiness, or lack of humility, or whatever the fault was. I must humble myself before God for the fault; but then it is very pride and a still worse fault to go on fidgeting about the forgiven fault, calling myself all the bad names in the dictionary. It may be quite true in fact, but it is not true in humility and gratitude for God's love of me a sinner, to go on dwelling upon my badness, the obstinate contemplation of which shuts out the sight of God's goodness and beauty. . . . I am very glad if it may possibly be that my fault may do good somehow to someone else, because God overrules evil for good; but the evil is not God's work but mine. But if I am sorry and own it, I will not dwell on it as if evil were the victorious power, but will thank God for His pardoning love, and try to be

more humble and simple, and to keep my spirit in obedience to the
Spirit of Christ for the future. It is possible to go on simply, and
avoid a thousand perplexing questions, pains and doubts, which
are unnecessary and unreal. It is possible because we can learn to
abide in Christ more closely, and so to be subject to His wise and
gracious inspiration, instead of at the mercy of our own tempests.

—G. CONGREVE

October 6

*May the God of peace . . . equip you with everything good
for doing his will . . .*
HEBREWS 13:20-21

*Be strong!
We are not here to play, to dream, to drift;
We have hard work to do and loads to lift;
Shun not the struggle – face it; 'tis God's gift.*
MALTBIE DAVENPORT BABCOCK

It would seem that Our Lord finds our desires not too strong,
but too weak. We are half-hearted creatures, fooling about with
drink and sex and ambition when infinite joy is offered us, like
an ignorant child who wants to go on making mud pies in a slum
because he cannot imagine what is meant by the offer of a holiday
at the sea. We are far too easily pleased.

—C.S. LEWIS

October 7

*The plans of the diligent lead to profit
as surely as haste leads to poverty.*
PROVERBS 21:5

*The best things are never arrived at in haste.
God is in no hurry; His plans are never rushed.*
MICHAEL PHILLIPS

The scenes in our life resemble pictures in a rough mosaic; they are ineffective from close up, and have to be viewed from a distance if they are to seem beautiful. That is why to attain something desired is to discover how vain it is; and why, though we live all our lives in expectation of better things, we often at the same time long regretfully for what is past. The present, on the other hand, is regarded as something quite temporary and serving as the only road to our goal. That is why most men discover when they look back on their life that they have been living the whole time ad interim, and are surprised to see that which they let go by so unregarded and unenjoyed was precisely their life, was precisely that in expectation of which they lived.

—ARTHUR SCHOPENHAUER

October 8

But you will not leave in haste or go in flight;
for the Lord will go before you . . .
ISAIAH 52:12

Holy Spirit, Peace divine!
Still this restless heart of mine;
Speak to calm this tossing sea,
Stayed in Thy tranquility.
S. LONGFELLOW

In whatever you are called upon to do, endeavor to maintain a
calm, collected, and prayerful state of mind. Self-recollection is
of great importance. "It is good for a man to quietly wait for the
salvation of the Lord." He who is in what may be called a spiritual
hurry, or rather who runs without having evidence of being
spiritually sent, makes haste to no purpose.

—T. C. UPHAM

Haste, haste, has no blessing.

—ANONYMOUS PROVERB

He who brings trouble on his family will inherit only wind . . .
PROVERBS 11:29

. . . for there is nothing greater and better than this— when a
husband and wife keep a household in oneness of mind, a great woe
to their enemies and joy to their friends and win high renown.

—HOMER

The family, like the home in which they live, needs to be kept in
repair, lest some little rift in the walls should appear and let in the
wind and rain. The happiness of a family depends very much on
attention to little things. Order, comfort, regularity, cheerfulness,
good taste, pleasant conversation —these are the ornaments
of daily life, deprived of which it degenerates into a wearisome
routine. There must be light in the dwelling, and brightness and
pure spirits and cheerful smiles. Home is not usually the place of
toil, but the place to which we return and rest from our labors; in
which parents and children meet together and pass a joyful and
careless hour . . . Sympathy, too, is the noblest exercise; of it is the
Spirit of God working together with our spirit; it is warmth as well
as light, putting into us a new heart, and taking away the stony
heart which is dead to its natural surroundings.

—BENJAMIN JOWETT

October 10

. . . there is a future for the man of peace.
PSALMS 37:37

In the heart's depths a peace serene and holy
Abides, and when pain seems to have its will,
Or we despair,—oh, may that peace rise slowly,
Stronger than agony, and we be still.
SAMUEL JOHNSON

May today there be peace within. May you trust that you are exactly where you are meant to be. May you not forget the infinite possibilities that are born of faith in yourself and others. May you use the gifts that you have received, and pass on the love that has been given to you. May you be content with yourself just the way you are. Let this knowledge settle into your bones, and allow your soul the freedom to sing, dance, praise and love. It is there for each and every one of us.

—SAINT TERESE OF LISEAUX

October 11

Blessed are the peacemakers,
for they will be called sons of God.
MATTHEW 5:9

Love all, trust a few, do wrong to none.
SHAKESPEARE

Forgiveness is the name of love practiced among people who love poorly. The hard truth is that all people love poorly. We need to forgive and be forgiven every day, every hour increasingly. That is the great work of love among the fellowship of the weak that is the human family.

—HENRI J.M. NOUWEN

October 12

They will enter Zion with singing;
everlasting joy will crown their heads. Gladness and joy will overtake
them, and sorrow and sighing will flee away.
ISAIAH 51:11

But if you love and must needs have desires,
let these be your desires:
To melt and be like a running brook that
sings its melody to the night.
To know the pain of too much tenderness.
To be wounded by your own understanding of love;
And to bleed willingly and joyfully.
To wake at dawn with a winged heart and
give thanks for another day of loving;
To rest at noon hour and meditate love's ecstasy;
To return home at eventide with gratitude;
And then to sleep with a prayer for the beloved in your heart and
a song of praise on your lips.
KHALIL GIBRAN

Love, Joy, Peace, Patience, Kindness, Goodness, Faithfulness, Gentleness, and Self-Control. To these I commit my day. If I succeed, I will give thanks. If I fail, I will seek His grace. And then when this day is done I will place my head on my pillow and rest.

—MAX LUCADO

October 13

We want each of you to show this same diligence to the very end, in order to make your hope sure. We do not want you to become lazy . . .
HEBREWS 6:11-12

When I am assailed with heavy tribulations, I rush out among my pigs rather than remain alone by myself. The human heart is like a millstone in a mill: when you put wheat under it, it turns and grinds and bruises the wheat to flour; if you put no wheat, it still grinds on, but then 'tis itself it grinds and wears away. So the human heart, unless it be occupied with some employment, leaves space for the devil, who wriggles himself in and brings with him a whole host of evil thoughts, temptations, and tribulations, which grind out the heart.

—MARTIN LUTHER

There is nothing noble in being superior to your fellow man; true nobility is being superior to your former self.

—ERNEST HEMINGWAY

October 14

And forgive your people who have sinned against you.
2 CHRONICLES 6:39

> *Hark! the herald angels sing*
> *Glory to the newborn King;*
> *Peace on earth and mercy mild*
> *God and sinners reconciled!*
> CHARLES WESLEY

Forgiveness is not about forgetting. It is about letting go of another person's throat. . . Forgiveness does not create a relationship. Unless people speak the truth about what they have done and change their mind and behavior, a relationship of trust is not possible. When you forgive someone you certainly release them from judgment, but without true change, no real relationship can be established. . .Forgiveness in no way requires that you trust the one you forgive. But should they finally confess and repent, you will discover a miracle in your own heart that allows you to reach out and begin to build between you a bridge of reconciliation. . .Forgiveness does not excuse anything. . .You may have to declare your forgiveness a hundred times the first day and the second day, but the third day will be less and each day after, until one day you will realize that you have forgiven completely. And then one day you will pray for his wholeness. . . .

—W. PAUL YOUNG

For sin shall not be your master,
because you are not under law, but under grace.
ROMANS 6:14

The truth is, unless you let go, unless you forgive yourself,
unless you forgive the situation, unless you realize that that
situation is over, you cannot move forward.
RUTILIUS

Yes, this sin which has sent me wearyhearted to bed and desperate
in heart to morning work, that has made my plans miscarry until
I am a coward, that cuts me off from prayer, that robs the sky of
blueness and the earth of spring-time, and the air of freshness,
and human faces of friendliness—this blasting sin which perhaps
has made my bed in hell for me so long—this can be conquered. I
do not say annihilated, but, better than that, conquered, captured
and transfigured into a friend: so that I at last shall say, "My
temptation has become my strength! for to the very fight with it I
owe my force."

—W. C. GANNETT

October 16

Let us fall into the hands of the Lord, for his mercy is great . . .
2 SAMUEL 24:14

The quality of mercy is not strain'd
It droppeth as the gentle rain from heaven
Upon the place beneath: it is twice bless'd;
It blesseth him that gives and him that takes:
'Tis mightiest in the mightiest; it becomes
The throned monarch better than his crown;
His scepter shows the force of temporal power,
The attribute to awe and majesty,
Wherein doth sit the dread and fear of kings;
But mercy is above this sceptered sway,
It is enthroned in the hearts of kings,
It is an attribute to God himself,
And earthly power doth then show likest God's
When mercy seasons justice . . . we do pray for mercy,
And that same prayer doth teach us all to render
The deeds of mercy.
WILLIAM SHAKESPEARE

We hand folks over to God's mercy, and show none ourselves.
—GEORGE ELIOT

Who will not mercy unto others show, how can he mercy ever hope to have?
—EDMUND SPENSER

October 17

*Walk in his ways, and keep his decrees and commands, his laws
and requirements, as written in the Law of Moses, so that you may
prosper in all you do and wherever you go . . .*
1 KINGS 2:3

Dearest Lord, teach me to be generous;
Teach me to serve thee as thou deservest;
To give and not to count the cost,
To fight and not to heed the wounds,
To toil and not to seek for rest,
To labor and not to seek reward,
Save that of knowing that I do thy will.
ST. IGNATIUS LOYOLA

When I despair, I remember that all through history the way of
truth and love have always won. There have been tyrants and
murderers, and for a time, they can seem invincible, but in the end,
they always fall. Think of it—always.

—MAHATMA GANDHI

It is not the multitude of hard duties, it is not constraint and
contention that advance us in our Christian course. On the
contrary, it is the yielding of our wills without restriction and
without choice, to tread cheerfully every day in the path in which
Providence leads us, to seek nothing, to be discouraged by nothing,
to see our duty in the present moment, to trust all else without
reserve to the will and power of God.

—FENELON

October 18

Now strengthen my hands.
NEHEMIAH 6:9

Be strong, live happy, and love, but first of all
Him whom to love is to obey, and keep
His great command; take heed lest passion sway
Thy judgment to do aught which else free will
Would not admit; thine and of all thy sons
The weal or woe in thee is placed; beware.
I in thy persevering shall rejoice,
And all the blest. Stand fast; to stand or fall
Free in thine own arbitrement it lies.
Perfect within, no outward aid require;
And all temptation to transgress repel.
JOHN MILTON

You perhaps will say that all people fall short of the perfection
of the Gospel, and therefore you are content with your failings.
But this is saying nothing to the purpose: for the question is not
whether Gospel perfection can be fully attained, but whether you
come as near it as a sincere intention and careful diligence can
carry you. Whether you are not in a much lower state than you
might be if you sincerely intended and carefully labored to advance
yourself in all Christian virtues.

—WILLIAM LAW

October 19

In all your ways acknowledge him,
and he will make your paths straight.
PROVERBS 3:6

Of all paths a man could strike into, there is, at any given moment, a best path for every man; a thing which, here and now, it were of all things wisest for him to do; which could he but be led or driven to do, he were then doing "like a man," as we phrase it. His success, in such case, were complete, his felicity a maximum. This path, to find this path, and walk in it, is the one thing needful for him.

—THOMAS CARLYLE

Every man has his own vocation. There is one direction in which all space is open to him. He has faculties silently inviting him thither to endless exertion. He is like a ship in a river; he runs against obstructions on every side but one; on that side all obstruction is taken away, and he sweeps serenely over a deepening channel into an infinite sea.

—RALPH WALDO EMERSON

Do not be overcome with evil, but overcome evil with good.
ROMANS 12:21

'Tis the human touch in this world that counts,
The touch of your hand and mine,
Which means far more to the fainting heart
Than shelter and bread and wine;
For shelter is gone when the night is o'er,
And bread lasts only a day,
But the touch of the hand and the sound of the voice
Sing on in the soul alway.
SPENCER MICHAEL FREE

If we wish to overcome evil, we must overcome it by good. There are doubtless many ways of overcoming the evil in our own hearts, but the simplest, easiest, most universal, is to overcome it by active occupation in some good word or work. The best antidote against evil of all kinds, against the evil thoughts which haunt the soul, against the needless perplexities which distract the conscience, is to keep hold of the good we have. Impure thoughts will not stand against pure words, and prayers, and deeds. Little doubts will not avail against great certainties. Fix your affections on things above, and then you will be less and less troubled by the cares, the temptations, the troubles of things on earth.

—A. P. STANLEY

October 21

I will be careful to lead a blameless life . . .
PSALMS 101:2

How happy is the blameless vestal's lot!
The world forgetting, by the world forgot.
Eternal sunshine of the spotless mind!
Each pray'r accepted, and each wish resign'd;
Labour and rest, that equal periods keep;
Obedient slumbers that can wake and weep.
ALEXANDER POPE

The reason to forgive ourselves is not because we feel like it or because we want to see ourselves as blameless but because we limit what we can receive from God when we hold on to our past. He wants to do so much more than we could ever imagine. Forgiving yourself starts with believing in God's incredible love for you and accepting His amazing grace and mercy. If God Almighty can forgive us who are we to hold on to what He has not only forgiven but forgotten.

—SUE AUGUSTINE

October 22

Be joyful always, pray continually; give thanks in all circumstances,
for this is God's will for you in Christ Jesus.
1 THESSALONIANS 5:16-18

To fret thy soul with crosses and with cares;
To eat thy heart through comfortless despairs;
To fawn, to crouch, to wait, to ride, to run,
To spend, to give, to want, to be undone.
Unhappy wight, born to disastrous end,
That doth his life in so long tendance spend.

EDMUND SPENSER

Anyone who imagines that bliss is normal is going to waste a lot of time running around shouting that he has been robbed. The fact is that most putts don't drop, most beef is tough, most children grow up to be just like people, most successful marriages require a high degree of mutual toleration, and most jobs are more often dull than otherwise. Life is just like an old time rail journey. . . delays, sidetracks, smoke, dust, cinders, and jolts, interspersed only occasionally by beautiful vistas and thrilling bursts of speed. The trick is to thank the Lord for letting you have the ride.

—JENKIN LLOYD JONES

October 23

Teach me to do your will, for you are my God;
may your good Spirit lead me on level ground.

PSALMS 143:10

Just as Thou wilt is just what I would will;
Give me but this, the heart to be content,
And, if my wish is thwarted, to lie still,
Waiting till puzzle and till pain are spent,
And the sweet thing made plain which the Lord meant.

SUSAN COOLIDGE

The best way to not feel hopeless is to get up and do something. Don't wait for good things to happen to you. If you go out and make some good things happen, you will fill the world with hope, you will fill yourself with hope.

—BARACK OBAMA

October 24

But let all who take refuge in you be glad; let them ever sing for joy. Spread your protection over them, that those who love your name may rejoice in you. For surely, Oh Lord, you bless the righteous; you surround them with your favor as with a shield.

PSALMS 5:11-12

Courage is fear that has said its prayers
and decided to go forward anyway.

JOYCE MEYER

Lord, protect our decisions, because making Decision is a way of praying. Give us the courage after our doubts, to be able to choose between one road and another. May our YES always be a YES and our NO always be a NO. Once we have chosen our road, may we never look back nor allow our soul to be eaten away by remorse. And in order for this to be possible.

—PAULO COELHO

October 25

And earth has nothing I desire besides you. My flesh and my heart may fail, but God is the strength of my heart and my portion forever.
PSALMS 73:25-26

*Love is seeing God in the person next to us;
meditation is seeing God within us.*
SRI SRI RAVI SHANKAR

Be of good faith, my dear Friends, look not out at any thing; fear none of those things ye may be exposed to suffer, either outwardly or inwardly; but trust the Lord over all, and your life will spring, and grow, and refresh you, and ye will learn obedience and faithfulness daily more and more, even by your exercises and sufferings; yea, the Lord will teach you the very mystery of faith and obedience; the wisdom, power, love, and goodness of the Lord ordering every thing for you, and ordering your hearts in everything.

—I. PENINGTON

. . . in quietness and trust is your strength . . .
ISAIAH 30:15

O Power to do; O baffled will!
O prayer and action! ye are one.
Who may not strive, may yet fulfil
The harder task of standing still,
And good but wished with God is done.
J. G. WHITTIER

I must say a word about fear. It is life's only true opponent. Only fear can defeat life. It is a clever, treacherous adversary, how well I know. It has no decency, respects no law or convention, shows no mercy. It goes for your weakest spot, which it finds with unnerving ease. It begins in your mind, always ... so you must fight hard to express it. You must fight hard to shine the light of words upon it. Because if you don't, if your fear becomes a wordless darkness that you avoid, perhaps even manage to forget, you open yourself to further attacks of fear because you never truly fought the opponent who defeated you.

—YANN MARTEL

My grace is sufficient for you, my power is made perfect in your weakness. That is why, for Christ's sake, I delight in weaknesses, in insults, in hardships, in persecutions, in difficulties. For when I am weak, then I am strong.

2 CORINTHIANS 12:9-10

To suffer woes which Hope thinks infinite;
To forgive wrongs darker than death or night;
To defy Power, which seems omnipotent;
To love, and bear; to hope till Hope creates
From its own wreck the thing it contemplates;
Neither to change, nor falter, nor repent;
This, like thy glory, Titan, is to be
Good, great and joyous, beautiful and free;
This is alone Life, Joy, Empire, and Victory.

PERCY BYSSHE SHELLEY

These really are our days, and we can prevail and overcome, even in the midst of trends that are very disturbing. If we are faithful the day will come when those deserving pioneers and ancestors, whom we rightly praise for having overcome the adversities in the wilderness trek, will praise today's faithful for having made their way successfully through a desert of despair and for having passed through a cultural wilderness, while still keeping the faith.

—NEAL A. MAXWELL

October 28

How precious to me are your thoughts, O God!
How vast is the sum of them!
Were I to count them they would
outnumber the grains of sand.

PSALMS 139:17-18

Thy thoughts are good, and Thou art kind,
Even when we think it not;
How many an anxious, faithless mind
Sits grieving o'er its lot,
And frets, and pines by day and night,
As God had lost it out of sight,
And all its wants forgot.

P. GERHARDT

To be hopeful in bad times is not just foolishly romantic. It is based on the fact that human history is a history not only of cruelty, but also of compassion, sacrifice, courage, kindness.

What we choose to emphasize in this complex history will determine our lives. If we see only the worst, it destroys our capacity to do something. If we remember those times and places—and there are so many—where people have behaved magnificently, this gives us the energy to act, and at least the possibility of sending this spinning top of a world in a different direction.

And if we do act, in however small a way, we don't have to wait for some grand utopian future. The future is an infinite succession of presents, and to live now as we think human beings should live, in defiance of all that is bad around us, is itself a marvelous victory.

—HOWARD ZINN

Be joyful in hope,
patient in affliction,
faithful in prayer.
ROMANS 12:12

Nine requisites for contented living:
Health enough to make work a pleasure.
Wealth enough to support your needs.
Strength to battle with difficulties and overcome them.
Grace enough to confess your sins and forsake them.
Patience enough to toil until some good is accomplished.
Charity enough to see some good in your neighbor.
Love enough to move you to be useful and helpful to others.
Faith enough to make real the things of God.
Hope enough to remove all anxious fears concerning the future.
JOHANN WOLFGANG VON GOETHE

No pain that we suffer, no trial that we experience is wasted. It ministers to our education, to the development of such qualities as patience, faith, fortitude and humility. All that we suffer and all that we endure, especially when we endure it patiently, builds up our characters, purifies our hearts, expands our souls, and makes us more tender and charitable, more worthy to be called the children of God . . . and it is through sorrow and suffering, toil and tribulation, that we gain the education that we come here to acquire and which will make us more like our Father and Mother in heaven.

—ORSON F. WHITNEY

Guard the good deposit that was entrusted to you—guard it with the help of the Holy Spirit who lives in us.
2 TIMOTHY 1:14

Love is the "why" of life,
why we are functioning at all.
I am convinced
it is the fundamental energy
of the human spirit.
the fuel on which we run,
the wellspring of our vitality.

And grace,
which is the flowing,
creative activity, of love itself,
is what makes all goodness possible.

Love should come first,
it should be the beginning of,
and the reason for everything.
GERALD G. MAY

We do not believe in ourselves until someone reveals that deep inside us something is valuable, worth listening to, worthy of our trust, sacred to our touch. Once we believe in ourselves we can risk curiosity, wonder, spontaneous delight or any experience that reveals the human spirit.

—E.E. CUMMINGS

October

October 31

Whoever finds his life will lose it,
and whoever loses his life for my sake will find it.
MATTHEW 10:39

No coward soul is mine,
No trembler in the world's storm-troubled sphere:
I see Heaven's glories shine,
And faith shines equal arming me from fear . . . .
There is not room for Death.
Nor atom that his might could render void:
Thou—Thou art Being and Breath,
And what Thou art may never be destroyed.
EMILY BRONTE

Be of good cheer about death, and know this of a truth, that no evil
can happen to a good man, either in life or after death.

—SOCRATES

November

November 1

In my Father's house are many rooms; if it were not so, I would have told you. I am going there to prepare a place for you."
JOHN 14:2

Consequently, you are no longer foreigners and aliens, but fellow citizens with God's people and members of God's household . . .
EPHESIANS 2:19

My church has but one temple,
Wide as the world is wide,
Set with a million stars,
Where a million hearts abide.

My church has no creed to bar
A single brother man
But says, "Come thou and worship"
To everyone who can.

My church has no roof or walls,
Nor floors save the beautiful sod—
For fear, I would seem to limit
The love of the illimitable God.
E. O. G.

We who practice the Christian tradition understand [Jesus Christ] as our vehicle to the divine. But for us to assume that God could not act in other ways is, I think, to put God in an awfully small box.

—KATHARINE JEFFERTS SCHORI

Therefore, since we are surrounded by such a great cloud of witnesses, let us throw off everything that hinders and the sin that so easily entangles, and let us run with perseverance the race marked out for us.
HEBREWS 12:1

We need more light about each other. Light creates understanding, understanding creates love, love creates patience, and patience creates unity.

—MALCOLM X

"He went about doing good." So we might say in our own age of two or three who have been personally known to us, "He or she went about doing good." They are the living witnesses to us of His work. If we observe them we shall see that they did good because they were good—because they lived for others and not for themselves, because they had a higher standard of truth and therefore men could trust them, because their love was deeper and therefore they drew others after them. These are they of whom we read in Scripture that they bear the image of Christ until His coming again, and of a few of them that they have borne the image of His sufferings, and to us they are the best interpreters of His life.

—BENJAMIN JOWETT

November 3

Therefore each of you must put off falsehood and speak truthfully to his neighbor, for we are all members of one body.
EPHESIANS 4:25

You shall not give false testimony against your neighbor.
EXODUS 20:16

What the superior man seeks is in himself;
what the small man seeks is in others.
CONFUCIUS

We begin, I think, when we set out to lie and deceive, by having an increased sense of power. . . . I suppose the successful liar may continue to enjoy this feeling of triumph and superiority, so that he does not notice what is happening to him. But something very terrible is happening. The lie does not stay outside his soul; it does not remain the mere instrument used so cleverly by the self; it invades the self and becomes part of it. I have heard that actors who have played one part for a long time sometimes become temporarily deranged and cannot distinguish their real selves from the person whom they were representing in the drama. Something of the same kind happens to the man who has cultivated insincerity, but his is not a temporary derangement. . . . What has happened to him? He has lost the power to know himself, and with it the power to repent, unless the grace of God should, in some flash of revelation, dissolve the blinding veil he has bound upon his own eyes. One who cannot know himself cannot repent—that is why the Heavenly City includes none "that loveth or maketh a lie."
—W. R. MATTHEWS

November 4

Be wise in the way you act toward outsiders; make the most of every opportunity. Let your conversation be always full of grace, seasoned with salt, so that you may know how to answer everyone.

COLOSSIANS 4:5-6

If ever you have look'd on better days,
If ever been where bells have knoll'd to church,
If ever sat at any good man's feast,
If ever from your eyelids wip'd a tear,
And know what 'tis to pity, and be pitied,
Let gentleness my strong enforcement be.

WILLIAM SHAKESPEARE

In the end, we will remember not the words of our enemies, but the silence of our friends.

—MARTIN LUTHER KING, JR.

Injuries hurt not more in the receiving than in the remembrance. A small injury shall go as it comes; a great injury may dine or sup with me; but none at all shall lodge with me. Why should I vex myself because another hath vexed me? Grief for things past that cannot be remedied, and care for things to come that cannot be prevented, may easily hurt, can never benefit me. I will therefore commit myself to God in both, and enjoy the present.

—JOSEPH HALL

For we are the temple of the living God.
2 CORINTHIANS 6:16

We light the oven so that everyone may bake bread in it.
JOSE MARTI

I think all Christians would agree with me if I said that though Christianity seems at first to be all about morality, all about duties and rules and guilt and virtue, yet it leads you on, out of all that, into something beyond. One has a glimpse of a country where they do not talk of those things, except perhaps as a joke. Everyone there is filled full with what we should call goodness as a mirror is filled with light. But they do not call it goodness. They do not call it anything. They are not thinking of it. They are too busy looking at the source from which it comes. But this is near the stage where the road passes over the rim of our world. No one's eyes can see very far beyond that: lots of people's eyes can see further than mine.

—C.S. LEWIS

Evening, morning and noon, I cry out in distress,
and he hears my voice.
PSALMS 55:17

Speak to Him thou for He hears, and Spirit with
Spirit can meet—
Closer is He than breathing, and nearer than
hands and feet.
LORD ALFRED TENNYSON

Men and women who turn their lives over to God will discover that He can make a lot more out of their lives than they can. He can deepen their joys, expand their vision, quicken their minds, strengthen their muscles, lift their spirits, multiply their blessings, increase their opportunities, comfort their souls, and pour out peace.

—EZRA TAFT BENSON

For God does speak— now one way,
now another—though man may not perceive it.
JOB 33:14

God moves in a mysterious way,
His wonders to perform;
He plants his footsteps in the sea,
And rides upon the storm.
Deep in unfathomable mines
Of never-failing skill,
He treasures up his bright designs,
And works his sovereign will. . . .
WILLIAM COWPER

. . . In this state of universal uncertainty, where a thousand dangers hover about us, and none can tell whether the good that he pursues is not evil in disguise, or whether the next step will lead him to safety or destruction, nothing can afford any rational tranquility but the conviction that, however we amuse ourselves with unideal sounds, nothing in reality is governed by chance, but that the universe is under the perpetual superintendence of Him who created it; that our being is in the hands of omnipotent Goodness, by whom what appears casual to us is directed for ends ultimately kind and merciful; and that nothing can finally hurt him who debars not himself from the divine favor.

—SAMUEL JOHNSON

Here I am, I have come to do your will.
HEBREWS 10:9

There is no chance, no destiny, no fate,
Can circumvent or hinder or control
The firm resolve of a determined soul.
Gifts count for nothing; will alone is great;
Each wellborn soul must win what it deserves.
Let the fool prate of luck. The fortunate
Is he whose earnest purpose never swerves,
Whose slightest action or inaction serves
The one great aim. Why, even Death stands still,
And waits an hour sometimes for such a will.
ELLA WHEELER WILCOX

Whatever you are physically. . . male or female, strong or weak, ill or healthy—all those things matter less than what your heart contains. If you have the soul of a warrior, you are a warrior. All those other things, they are the glass that contains the lamp, but you are the light inside.

—CASSANDRA CLARE

We either make ourselves miserable, or we make ourselves strong. The amount of work is the same.

— CARLOS CASTANEDA

November 9

*The Lord, the Lord, the compassionate and gracious God . . .
maintaining love to thousands, and forgiving wickedness,
rebellion and sin.*
EXODUS 34:6-7

Be kind, for everyone you meet is fighting a harder battle.
PLATO

I believe compassion to be one of the few things we can practice
that will bring immediate and long-term happiness to our lives. I'm
not talking about the short-term gratification of pleasures like sex,
drugs or gambling (though I'm not knocking them), but something
that will bring true and lasting happiness. The kind that sticks.
—DALAI LAMA XIV

November 10

*You have made known to me the path of life;
you will fill me with joy . . .*
PSALMS 16:11

Face your life, its pain, its pleasure, leave no path untaken.
NEIL GAIMAN

Words can never fully say what we want them to say, for they
fumble, stammer, and break the best porcelain. The best one
can hope for is to find along the way someone to share the path,
content to walk in silence, for the heart communes best when it
does not try to speak.

—MARGARET WEIS

November 11

*And we pray this in order that you may live a life worthy of the
Lord and may please him in every way:
bearing fruit in every good work . . .*
COLOSSIANS 1:10

Do not confuse "duty" with what other people expect of you; they
are utterly different. Duty is a debt you owe to yourself to fulfill
obligations you have assumed voluntarily. Paying that debt can
entail anything from years of patient work to instant willingness to
die. Difficult it may be, but the reward is self-respect.

But there is no reward at all for doing what other people
expect of you, and to do so is not merely difficult, but impossible.
It is easier to deal with a footpad than it is with the leech who
wants "just a few minutes of your time, please—this won't take
long." Time is your total capital, and the minutes of your life are
painfully few. If you allow yourself to fall into the vice of agreeing
to such requests, they quickly snowball to the point where these
parasites will use up 100 percent of your time—and squawk for
more!

So learn to say No—and to be rude about it when necessary.
Otherwise you will not have time to carry out your duty, or to do

your own work, and certainly no time for love and happiness. The termites will nibble away your life and leave none of it for you.

—ROBERT A. HEINLEIN

November 12

As long as it is day, we must do the work of him who sent me. Night is coming, when no one can work.
JOHN 9:4

He who intermits
The appointed task and duties of the day
Untunes full oft the pleasures of the day
Checking the finer spirits that refuse
To flow, when purposes are lightly changed.
WILLIAM WORDSWORTH

I've come to believe that each of us has a personal calling that's as unique as a fingerprint—and that the best way to succeed is to discover what you love and then find a way to offer it to others in the form of service, working hard, and also allowing the energy of the universe to lead you.

—OPRAH WINFREY

I'm a greater believer in luck, and I find the harder I work the more I have of it.

—THOMAS JEFFERSON

Blessed is the man you discipline, O Lord, the man you teach from your law; you grant him relief from days of trouble . . .
PSALMS 94:12-13

> *Then welcome each rebuff*
> *That turns earth's smoothness rough,*
> *Each sting that bids nor sit nor stand, but go!*
> *Be our joys three parts pain!*
> *Strive, and hold cheap the strain;*
> *Learn, nor account the pang; dare, never grudge*
> *the throe!*
> ROBERT BROWNING

With time and perspective we recognize that such problems in life do come for a purpose, if only to allow the one who faces such despair to be convinced that he really does need divine strength beyond himself, that she really does need the offer of heaven's hand. Those who feel no need for mercy usually never seek it and almost never bestow it. Those who have never had a heartache or a weakness or felt lonely or forsaken never have had to cry unto heaven for relief of such personal pain. Surely it is better to find the goodness of God and the grace of Christ, even at the price of despair, than to risk living our lives in a moral or material complacency that has never felt any need for faith or forgiveness, any need for redemption or relief.

—JEFFERY R. HOLLAND

Do not run to this and that for comfort when you are in trouble, but bear it. Be uncomfortably quiet—be uneasily silent—be patiently unhappy.

—J. P. GREAVES

November 14

I am the Lord your God, who teaches you what is best for you, who directs you in the way you should go.
ISAIAH 48:17

What's in store for me in the direction I don't take?
JACK KEROUAC

Choosing a path meant having to miss out on others. She had a whole life to live, and she was always thinking that, in the future, she might regret the choices she made now. "I'm afraid of committing myself," she thought to herself. She wanted to follow all possible paths and so ended up following none. Even in that most important area of her life, love, she had failed to commit herself. After her first romantic disappointment, she had never again given herself entirely. She feared pan, loss, and separation. These things were inevitable on the path to love, and the only way of avoiding them was by deciding not to take that path at all. In order not to suffer, you had to renounce love. It was like putting out your own eyes not to see the bad things in life.

—PAULO COELHO

So do not fear, for I am with you; do not be dismayed
for I am your God. I will strengthen you and help you;
I will uphold you with my righteous right hand.

ISAIAH 41:10

I long to accomplish a great and noble task, but it is my chief duty
to accomplish small tasks as if they were great and noble.

HELEN KELLER

Why is Dickens' "Christmas Carol" so popular? Why is it ever new? I personally feel it is inspired of God. It brings out the best within human nature. It gives hope. It motivates change. We can turn from the paths which would lead us down and, with a song in our hearts, follow a star and walk toward the light. We can quicken our step, bolster our courage, and bask in the sunlight of truth. We can hear more clearly the laughter of little children. We can dry the tear of the weeping. We can comfort the dying by sharing the promise of eternal life. If we lift one weary hand which hangs down, if we bring peace to one struggling soul, if we give as did the Master, we can—by showing the way—become a guiding star for some lost mariner.

—THOMAS S. MONSON

November 16

*You will keep in perfect peace him whose mind is steadfast,
because he trusts in you. Trust in the Lord forever, for the Lord,
the Lord, is the Rock eternal.*
ISAIAH 26:4

*Serene, I fold my hands and wait,
Nor care for wind, nor tide, nor sea;
I rave no more 'gainst time or fate,
For lo! my own shall come to me.*
JOHN BURROUGHS

Remember He is the artist and you are only the picture. You can't see it. So quietly submit to be painted—i.e., keep fulfilling all the obvious duties of your station (you really know quite well enough what they are!), asking forgiveness for each failure and then leaving it alone.You are in the right way. Walk—don't keep on looking at it.

—C.S. LEWIS

My mouth is filled with your praise,
declaring your splendor all day long.
PSALMS 71:8

For Equilibrium, a Blessing:
Like the joy of the sea coming home to shore,
May the relief of laughter rinse through your soul.

As the wind loves to call things to dance,
May your gravity by lightened by grace.

Like the dignity of moonlight restoring the earth,
May your thoughts incline with reverence and respect.

As water takes whatever shape it is in,
So free may you be about who you become.

As silence smiles on the other side of what's said,
May your sense of irony bring perspective.

As time remains free of all that it frames,
May your mind stay clear of all it names.

May your prayer of listening deepen enough
to hear in the depths the laughter of god.
JOHN O'DONOHUE

November 18

The mouth of the righteous is a fountain of life,
but violence overwhelms the mouth of the wicked.
PROVERBS 10:11

It is wise to direct your anger towards problems—not people; to
focus your energies on answers—not excuses.
WILLIAM ARTHUR WARD

Anybody can become angry—that is easy, but to be angry with
the right person and to the right degree and at the right time and
for the right purpose, and in the right way — that is not within
everybody's power and is not easy.

—ARISTOTLE

November 19

A fool's mouth is his undoing, and his lips are a snare to his soul.
PROVERBS 18:7

No sinful word, nor deed of wrong,
Nor thoughts that idly rove;
But simple truth be on our tongue,
And in our hearts be love.

ST. AMBROSE

The Wise Man observes that there is a time to speak and a time to keep silence. One meets with people in the world who seem never to have made the last of these observations. And yet these great talkers do not at all speak from their having anything to say, as every sentence shows, but only from their inclination to be talking. Their conversation is merely an exercise of the tongue: no other human faculty has any share in it. It is strange these persons can help reflecting that unless they have in truth a superior capacity, and are in an extraordinary manner furnished for conversation, if they are entertaining, they are entertaining at their own expense. Is it possible that it should never come into people's thoughts to suspect whether or no it be to their advantage to show so very much of themselves? Oh that you would altogether hold your peace, and it should be your wisdom! Remember likewise that there are persons who love fewer words, an inoffensive sort of people, and who deserve some regard, though of too still and composed tempers for you. . . .

—JOSEPH BUTLER

November 20

But hope that is seen is no hope at all.
Who hopes for what he already has? But if we hope
for what we do not yet have, we wait for it patiently.
ROMANS 8:24-25

"Hope" is the thing with feathers—
That perches in the soul—
And sings the tune without the words—
And never stops—at all.
EMILY DICKINSON

The very least you can do in your life is figure out what you hope for. And the most you can do is live inside that hope. Not admire it from a distance but live right in it, under its roof.

—BARBARA KINGSOLVER

November 21

It is written, 'Man does not live on bread alone,
but on every word that comes from the mouth of God.'
MATTHEW 4:4

Tamely, frail body, abstain today; today
My soul eats twice, Christ hither and away.
JOHN DONNE

We need or think we need a thousand things we could very well do without, and there are a thousand people importuning us to spend our money on them—thrusting them into our very hands on the most tempting terms. Plainly there are many people who find the temptation to spend so strong that they simply cannot keep their money in their pockets. It is drawn from them as by an irresistible attraction. They have no bad conscience about it, but they just do not know where it goes. It goes on dress, on traveling, on trinkets, on personal adornments, and indulgence of every kind . . . But the true moral of this is . . . that it is not the way to become rich toward God.

—JAMES DENNEY

Is that beast better, that hath two or three mountains to graze on, than a little bee, that feeds on dew or manna, and lives, upon what falls every morning from the storehouse of heaven, clouds, and providence?

—JEREMY TAYLOR

And when you pray, do not keep on babbling, like pagans, for they think they will be heard because of their many words. Do not be like them, for your Father knows what you need before you ask him.

MATTHEW 6:7-8

. . . Must helpless man, in ignorance sedate,
Roll darling down the torrent of his fate?
Must no dislike alarm, no wishes rise,
No cries invoke the mercies of the skies?
Inquirer, cease; petitions yet remain,
Which Heaven may hear, nor deem religion vain.
Still raise for good the supplicating voice,
But leave to Heaven the measure and the choice.
Safe in His power, whose eyes discern afar
The secret ambush of a specious prayer.
Implore His aid, in His decisions rest,
Secure, whate'er He gives, He gives the best . . .

SAMUEL JOHNSON

As soon as we are with God in faith and in love, we are in prayer.

—FENELON

Prayer is not asking. It is a longing of the soul. It is daily admission of one's weakness. It is better in prayer to have a heart without words than words without a heart.

—MAHATMA GANDHI

Blessed is the man who finds wisdom,
the man who gains understanding,
for she is more profitable than silver and
yields better returns than gold.

PROVERBS 3:13-14

O World, thou choosest not the better part!
It is not wisdom to be only wise,
And on the inward vision close the eyes,
But it is wisdom to believe the heart.

GEORGE SANTAYANA

To be ignorant of one's ignorance is the malady of the ignorant.

—AMOS BRONSON ALCOTT

Where there is charity and wisdom,
there is neither fear nor ignorance.
Where there is patience and humility,
there is neither anger nor vexation.
Where there is poverty and joy, t
here is neither greed nor avarice.
Where there is peace and meditation,
there is neither anxiety nor doubt.

ST. FRANCIS OF ASSISI

November 24

Be strong and take heart, all you who hope in the Lord.
PSALMS 31:24

In heavenly love abiding,
No change my heart shall fear
And safe is such confiding,
For nothing changes here.
A. L. WARING

The greatest disease in the West today is not TB or leprosy; it is being unwanted, unloved, and uncared for. We can cure physical diseases with medicine, but the only cure for loneliness, despair, and hopelessness is love. There are many in the world who are dying for a piece of bread but there are many more dying for a little love. The poverty in the West is a different kind of poverty—it is not only a poverty of loneliness but also of spirituality. There's a hunger for love, as there is a hunger for God.

—MOTHER TERESA

November 25

Be strong and courageous. Do not be afraid or terrified because of them, for the Lord your God goes with you; he will never leave you nor forsake you.
DEUTERONOMY 31:6

It is often in the darkest
skies that we see the
brightest stars.
RICHARD EVANS

The lessons of the moral sentiment are, once for all, an emancipation from that anxiety which takes the joy out of all life. It teaches a great peace. It comes itself from the highest place. It is that, which being in all sound natures, and strongest in the best and most gifted men, we know to be implanted by the Creator of men. It is a commandment at every moment, and in every condition of life, to do the duty of that moment, and to abstain from doing the wrong.

—RALPH WALDO EMERSON

November 26

I am with you and will watch over you wherever you go.
GENESIS 28:15

. . . he will watch over your life; the Lord will watch over your coming
and going, both now and forevermore.
PSALMS 121:7-8

I never spoke with God
Nor visited in Heaven—
Yet certain am I of the spot
As if the Checks were given . . .

EMILY DICKINSON

If there is no god, what is left but science? What is left to endow us with any grace? You can tell me the chemical makeup of my skin and my brain, but how can you explain away my soul? And if there is no god to watch over me, chastise me, grieve for me, rejoice for me, make me fear, and make me wonder, what am I but a collection of metals and liquids with nothing to celebrate about my daily living?

—SHARON SHINN

November 27

I was pushed back and about to fall, but the Lord helped me.
The Lord is my strength and my song; he has become my salvation.

PSALMS 118:13-14

My plea. . . is a plea to save the children. Too many of them walk with pain and fear, in loneliness and despair. Children need sunlight . . .They need kindness and refreshment and affection. Every home, regardless of the cost of the house, can provide an environment of love which will be an environment of salvation.

—GORDON B. HINCKLEY

You are told a lot about your education, but some beautiful, sacred memory, preserved since childhood, is perhaps the best education of all. If a man carries many such memories into life with him, he is saved for the rest of his days. And even if only one good memory is left in our hearts, it may also be the instrument of our salvation one day.

—FYODOR DOSTOYEVSKY

November 28

*. . . our God gives light to our eyes and
a little relief in our bondage . . . He has shown us kindness.*
EZRA 9:9

*The heart benevolent and kind
The most resembles God.*
ROBERT BURNS

What wisdom can you find that is greater than kindness?
—JEAN JACQUES ROUSSEAU

"Live each day as if it's your last," that was the conventional advice, but really, who had the energy for that? What if it rained or you felt a bit glandy? It just wasn't practical. Better by far to simply try and be good and courageous and bold and to make a difference. Not change the world exactly, but the bit around you. Go out there with your passion and your electric typewriter and work hard at... something. Change lives through art maybe. Cherish your friends, stay true to your principles, live passionately and fully and well. Experience new things. Love and be loved, if you ever get the chance.

—DAVID NICHOLLS

November 29

He chose David his servant and took him from the sheep pens; from tending the sheep he brought him to be the shepherd of his people. . . And David shepherded them with integrity of heart; with skillful hands he led them.
PSALMS 78:70-72

Integrity is doing the right thing, even when no one is watching.
C.S. LEWIS

Imagine life is a game in which you are juggling five balls. The balls are called work, family, health, friends, and integrity. And you're keeping all of them in the air. But one day you finally come to understand that work is a rubber ball. If you drop it, it will bounce back. The other four balls...are made of glass. If you drop one of these, it will be irrevocably scuffed, nicked, perhaps even shattered.

—JAMES PATTERSON

November 30

We are hard-pressed on every side, but not crushed; perplexed, but not in despair . . .
2 CORINTHIANS 4:8

OH my soul, why are thou vexed?
Let things go e'en as they will;
Though to thee they seem perplexed,
Yet His order they fulfil.
A. H. FRANCKE

The vexation, restlessness, and impatience which small trials cause, arise wholly from our ignorance and want of self-control. We may be thwarted and troubled, it is true, but these things put us into a condition for exercising patience and meek submission, and the self-abnegation wherein alone the fullness of God is to be found.

—DE RENTY

You live like this, sheltered, in a delicate world, and you believe you are living. Then you read a book… or you take a trip… and you discover that you are not living, that you are hibernating. The symptoms of hibernating are easily detectable: first, restlessness. The second symptom (when hibernating becomes dangerous and might degenerate into death): absence of pleasure. That is all. It appears like an innocuous illness. Monotony, boredom, death. Millions live like this (or die like this) without knowing it. They work in offices. They drive a car. They picnic with their families. They raise children. And then some shock treatment takes place, a person, a book, a song, and it awakens them and saves them from death. Some never awaken.

—ANAIS NIN

We need to find God, and he cannot be found in noise and restlessness. God is the friend of silence. See how nature - trees, flowers, grass- grows in silence; see the stars, the moon and the sun, how they move in silence… We need silence to be able to touch souls.

—MOTHER TERESA

December

December 1

> *Above all, love each other deeply, because love covers over a multitude of sins. Offer hospitality to one another without grumbling.*
> 1 PETER 4:8-9

If you want to live in the kind of a town
That's the kind of a town you like,
You needn't slip your clothes in a grip
And start on a long, long hike.

You'll find elsewhere what you left behind,
For there's nothing that's really new.
It's a knock at yourself when you knock your town;
It isn't your town—it's you.

Real towns are not made by men afraid
Lest somebody else gets ahead.
When everybody works and nobody shirks
You can raise a town from the dead.

And if while you make your stake
Your neighbor can make one, too,
Your town will be what you want to see,
It isn't your town—it's you.

R.W. GLOVER

If, on hearing of the fall of a brother, however differing or severed from us, we feel the least inclination to linger over it, instead of hiding it in grief and shame, or veiling it in the love which covereth

a multitude of sins; if, in seeing a joy or a grace or an effective
service given to others, we do not rejoice, but feel depressed, let us
be very watchful; the most diabolical of passions may mask itself as
humility, or zeal for the glory of God.

—ELIZABETH CHARLES

December 2

---

*You, therefore, have no excuse, you who pass judgment on someone
else, for at whatever point you judge the other, you are condemning
yourself, because you who pass judgment do the same things.*

ROMANS 2:1

If I knew you and you knew me—
If both of us could clearly see,
And with an inner sight divine
The meaning of your heart and mine—
I'm sure that we would differ less
And clasp our hands in friendliness;
Our thoughts would pleasantly agree
If I knew you, and you knew me.

If I knew you and you knew me,
As each one knows his own self, we
Could look each other in the face
And see therein a truer grace.
Life has so many hidden woes,
So many thorns for every rose;
The "why" of things our hearts would see,
If I knew you and you knew me.

NIXON WATERMAN

People hasten to judge in order not to be judged themselves.

—ALBERT CAMUS

December 3

---

*May the God of hope fill you with all joy and
peace as you trust in him, so that you may overflow with
hope by the power of the Holy Spirit.*

ROMANS 15:13

*I leant upon a coppice gate
When Frost was specter-gray,
And Winter's dregs made desolate
The weakening eye of day.
The tangled bine-stems scored the sky
Like strings of broken lyres,
and all mankind that haunted nigh
Had sought their household fires. . . .*

*At once a voice arose among
The bleak twigs overhead
In a full-hearted evensong
Of joy illimited;
An aged thrush, frail, gaunt, and small,
In blast-beruffled plume,
Had chosen thus to fling his soul
Upon the growing gloom.*

So little cause for carolings
Of such ecstatic sound
Was written on terrestrial things
Afar or nigh around,
That I could think there trembled through
His happy good-night air
Some blessed Hope, whereof he knew
And I was unaware.
THOMAS HARDY

You don't love someone because of their looks or their clothes or their car. You love them because they sing a song only your heart can understand.

—L.J. SMITH

December 4

Be strong and courageous. Do not be afraid or discouraged.
1 CHRONICLES 22:13

Let me do my work each day;
And if the darkened hours of despair overcome me,
May I not forget the strength that comforted me
In the desolation of other times.
May I still remember the bright hours that found me
Walking over the silent hills of my childhood,
Or dreaming on the margin of the quiet river,
When a light glowed within me,
And I promised my early God to have courage
Amid the tempests of the changing years. . . .
MAX EHRMANN

The brick walls are there for a reason. The brick walls are not there to keep us out. The brick walls are there to give us a chance to show how badly we want something. Because the brick walls are there to stop the people who don't want it badly enough. They're there to stop the other people.

—RANDY PAUSCH

December 5

May our Lord Jesus Christ himself and God our Father, who loved us and by his grace gave us eternal encouragement and good hope, encourage your hearts and strengthen you in every good deed and word.

THESSALONIANS 2:16

. . . Only Thou art above, and when towards Thee
By Thy leave I can look, I rise again;
But our old subtle foe so tempteth me
That not one hour myself I can sustain;
Thy grace may wing me to prevent his art,
And thou like adamant draw mine iron heart.

JOHN DONNE

Grace strikes us when we are in great pain and restlessness.
. Sometimes at that moment a wave of light breaks into our darkness, and it is as though a voice were saying: "You are accepted."

—PAUL TILLICH

Our chief want is someone who will inspire us to be what we know we could be.

—RALPH WALDO EMERSON

December 6

. . . for the Lord will be your confidence and
will keep your foot from being snared.
PROVERBS 3:26

Though I may stumble, I may fall,
My weakness is His strength;
No one is lost who hears His call:
His grace, my recompense.
E.C.M.

Success is stumbling from failure to failure with no loss of enthusiasm.

—WINSTON CHURCHILL

I will have nothing to do with a God who cares only occasionally. I need a God who is with us always, everywhere, in the deepest depths as well as the highest heights. It is when things go wrong, when good things do not happen, when our prayers seem to have been lost, that God is most present. We do not need the sheltering wings when things go smoothly. We are closest to God in the darkness, stumbling along blindly.

—MADELEINE L'ENGLE

December 7

Now we can see that you know all things and that you do not even need to have anyone ask you questions. This makes us believe that you came from God.

JOHN 16:30

Unite, My roving thoughts, unite
In silence soft and sweet;
And thou, my soul, sit gently down
At thy great Sovereign's feet.

P. DODDRIDGE

My wants seem to be gradually narrowing down, my personal wants, I mean, and I often think I could be quite content in the Poor-house! I do not know whether this is piety or old age, or a little of each mixed together, but honestly the world and our life in it does seem of too little account to be worth making the least fuss over, when one has such a magnificent prospect close at hand ahead of one; and I am tremendously content to let one activity after another go, and to await quietly and happily the opening of the door at the end of the passage way, that will let me in to my real abiding place. So you may think of me as happy and contented, surrounded with unnumbered blessings, and delighted to be seventy-one years old.

—MRS. PEARSALL SMITH

December 8

Blessed is the man who perseveres under trial, because when he has stood the test, he will receive the crown of life . . .

JAMES 1:12

How oft in this great city's din
Have I, my Savior, let you in?
Nor stopped nor paused amidst the fray
too busy e'er to kneel and pray.
But from my garden nature sings
Awake, my soul! remembering,
in chorus to join with the rest,
to thank God for His blessedness.

E. C. M.

The moment we begin to fear the opinions of others and hesitate to tell the truth that is in us, and from motives of policy are silent when we should speak, the divine floods of light and life no longer flow into our souls.

—ELIZABETH CADY STANTON

Things don't go wrong and break your heart so you can become bitter and give up. They happen to break you down and build you up so you can be all that you were intended to be.

—CHARLES JONES

December 9

*For with much wisdom comes much sorrow;
the more knowledge, the more grief.*
ECCLESIASTES 1:18

*I walked a mile with Pleasure;
She chattered all the way,
But left me none the wiser
For all she had to say.*

*I walked a mile with Sorrow
And ne'er a word said she;
But oh, the things I learned from her
When Sorrow walked with me!*
ROBERT BROWNING HAMILTON

In times of grief and sorrow I will hold you and rock you and take
your grief and make it my own. When you cry I cry and when you
hurt I hurt. And together we will try to hold back the floods to
tears and despair and make it through the potholed street of life.

—CORRIE TEN BOOM

He who heeds discipline shows the way to life,
but whoever ignores correction leads others astray.
PROVERBS 10:17

Love isn't something natural.
Rather it requires discipline, concentration,
patience, faith, and the overcoming of narcissism.
It isn't a feeling, it is a practice.
ERICH FROMM

The really important kind of freedom involves attention, and awareness, and discipline, and effort, and being able truly to care about other people and to sacrifice for them, over and over, in myriad petty little unsexy ways, every day.

—DAVID FOSTER WALLACE

Be not troubled; for if troubles abound, and there be tossing, and storms, and tempests, and no peace, nor anything visible left to support; yet, lie still, and sink beneath, till a secret hope stir, which will stay the heart in the midst of all these; until the Lord administer comfort, who knows how and what relief to give to the weary traveler, that knows not where it is, nor which way to look, nor where to expect a path.

—I. PENINGTON

December 11

Set your minds on things above,
not on earthly things.
COLOSSIANS 3:2

If everyone demanded peace instead of another television set,
then there'd be peace.
JOHN LENNON

You give but little when you give of your possessions. It is when you give of yourself that you truly give.

—KHALIL GIBRAN

We are not rich by what we possess but by what we can do without.
—IMMANUEL KANT

December 12

I desire to do your will, O my God, your law is within my heart.
PALMS 40:8

Thou that hast given so much to me,
Give one thing more, a grateful heart.
Not thankful when it pleaseth me,
As if thy blessings had spare days;
But such a heart, whose pulse may be
Thy praise.
GEORGE HERBERT

I would maintain that thanks are the highest form of thought; and that gratitude is happiness doubled by wonder.

—G.K. CHESTERTON

In the end, though, maybe we must all give up trying to pay back the people in this world who sustain our lives. In the end, maybe it's wiser to surrender before the miraculous scope of human generosity and to just keep saying thank you, forever and sincerely, for as long as we have voices.

— ELIZABETH GILBERT

Cultivate the habit of being grateful for every good thing that comes to you, and to give thanks continuously. And because all things have contributed to your advancement, you should include all things in your gratitude.

—RALPH WALDO EMERSON

December 13

I have learned the secret of being content in any and every situation, whether well fed or hungry, whether living in plenty or in want. I can do everything through him who gives me strength.
PHILIPPIANS 4:12-13

The greater part of our happiness or misery depends upon our dispositions, and not upon our circumstances.
MARTHA WASHINGTON

Actual happiness always looks pretty squalid in comparison with the overcompensations for misery. And, of course, stability isn't nearly so spectacular as instability. And being contented has none of the glamour of a good fight against misfortune, none of the picturesqueness of a struggle with temptation, or a fatal overthrow by passion or doubt. Happiness is never grand.

—ALDOUS HUXLEY

December 14

And what does the Lord require of you? To act justly and to love mercy and to walk humbly with your God.

MICAH 6:8

The mark of the immature man is that he wants to die nobly for a cause, while the mark of the mature man is that he wants to live humbly for one.

J.D. SALINGER

A mature person is one who does not think only in absolutes, who is able to be objective even when deeply stirred emotionally, who has learned that there is both good and bad in all people and in all things, and who walks humbly and deals charitably with the circumstances of life, knowing that in this world no one is all knowing and therefore all of us need both love and charity.

—ELEANOR ROOSEVELT

December 15

And he will be their peace.

MICAH 5:5

> *. . . Ere I am old, O! let me give*
> *My life to learning how to live;*
> *Then shall I meet with willing heart,*
> *An early summons to depart.*
> *Or find my lengthened days consoled*
> *By God's sweet peace—when I am old.*
> CAROLINE ATHERTON BRIGGS MASON

Love is the very essence of life. It is the pot of gold at the end of the rainbow. Yet it is not found only at the end of the rainbow. Love is at the beginning also, and from it springs the beauty that arched across the sky on a stormy day. Love is the security for which children weep, the yearning of youth, the adhesive that binds marriage, and the lubricant that prevents devastating friction in the home; it is the peace of old age, the sunlight of hope shining through death. How rich are those who enjoy it in their associations with family, friends, and neighbors! Love, like faith, is a gift of God. It is also the most enduring and most powerful virtue.

—GORDON B. HINKLEY

December 16

If I have the gift of prophecy and can fathom all mysteries and all knowledge, and if I have a faith that can move mountains, but have not love, I am nothing. If I give all I possess to the poor and surrender my body to the flames, but have not love, I gain nothing.

1 CORINTHIANS 13:2-3

Tis better to have loved and lost
Than never to have loved at all.

LORD ALFRED TENNYSON

If we do a thing because we think it is our duty, we generally fail; that is the old law which makes slaves of us. The real spring of our life, and of our work in life, must be love—true, deep love— not love of this or that person, or for this or that reason, but deep human love, devotion of soul to soul, love of God realized where alone it can be—in love of those whom He loves. Everything else is weak, passes away; that love alone supports us, makes life tolerable, binds the present together with the past and future, and is, we may trust, imperishable.

—MAX MULLER

December 17

*But the fruit of the Spirit is love, joy,
peace, patience, kindness,
goodness, faithfulness, gentleness and self-control.*
GALATIANS 5:22

Whoever is happy will make others happy too. He who has courage
and faith will never perish in misery!

—ANNE FRANK

We aim at something more sublime and more equitable—the
common good, or the community of goods. . . . We demand, we
would have, the communal enjoyment of the fruits of the earth,
fruits which are for everyone.

—FRANCOIS NOEL BABEUF, AKA "GRACCHUS"

The happiness of life is made up of minute fractions—the little
soon forgotten charities of a kiss or smile, a kind look, a heartfelt
compliment, and the countless infinitesimals of pleasurable and
genial feeling.

—SAMUEL TAYLOR COLERIDGE

There is no fear in love, but perfect love drives out fear.
1 JOHN 4:18

> *They sin who tell us love can die;*
> *With life all other passions fly,*
> *All others are but vanity.*
> ROBERT SOUTHEY

Would not the carrying out of one single commandment of Christ, "Love one another," change the whole aspect of the world, and sweep away prisons and workhouses, and envying and strife, and all the strongholds of the devil? Two thousand years have nearly passed, and people have not yet understood that one single command of Christ, "Love one another"!

—MAX MULLER

For one human being to love another human being: that is perhaps the most difficult task that has been given to us, the ultimate, the final problem and proof, the work for which all other work is merely preparation.

—RAINER MARIA RILKE

December 19

. . . let the wise listen and add to their learning.

PROVERBS 1:5

Hail to thee, blithe spirit!
Bird thou never wert,
That from heaven, or near it,
Pourest thy full heart
In profuse strains of unpremeditated art. . . .

Teach me half the gladness
That thy brain must know,
Such harmonious madness
From my lips would flow,
The world should listen then, as I am listening now.

PERCY BYSSHE SHELLEY

The attention of the listener serves as accompaniment to the music of the discourse. Everyone should be provided with that sort of indulgence, and that readiness to listen, which makes the thoughts of others bloom. It is a bad sort of cleverness which deprives the character of kindness, indulgence, and sympathy, which makes it difficult for us to live and talk with others, to make them pleased with us and pleased with themselves—in a word, to love and be lovable. The gentle mind is patient, gives itself without hurry to the task of understanding, is open to conviction, afraid of obstinacy, and would rather learn than take the lead.

—JOSEPH JOUBERT

December 20

*You need to persevere so that when you have done the will of God,
you will receive what he has promised.*
HEBREW 10:36

Living with integrity means: Not settling for less than what you
know you deserve in your relationships. Asking for what you want
and need from others. Speaking your truth, even though it might
create conflict or tension. Behaving in ways that are in harmony
with your personal values. Making choices based on what you
believe, and not what others believe.

—BARBARA DE ANGELIS

Resolved, that I will live so as I shall wish I had done when I come
to die. Resolved, never to speak in narrations anything but the pure
and simple verity.

—JONATHAN EDWARDS

"There is nothing," says Plato, "so delightful as the hearing or
the speaking of truth." For this reason there is no conversation so
agreeable as that of the man of integrity, who hears without any
intention to betray, and speaks without any intention to deceive.

—JOSEPH ADDISON

December 21

Teach me your way, O Lord, and I will walk in your truth.
PSALMS 86:11

All I have seen teaches me to trust the Creator
for all I have not seen.
RALPH WALDO EMERSON

What is a teacher? I'll tell you: it isn't someone who teaches something, but someone who inspires the student to give of her best in order to discover what she already knows.

—PAULO COELHO

Teach us to love without wanting to control; to love without limit; to love you, our friends, and also our enemies. Teach us to be patient in love when love is not returned; teach us to be patient when even you are apparently far away. Teach us loving, waiting, patience when there is no answer to our questionings and our doubt.

—MICHAEL HOLLINGS AND ETTA GULLICK

Who can discern his errors? Forgive my hidden faults.
PSALMS 19:12

> The night is come, like to the day,
> Depart not Thou, great God, away.
> Let not my sins, black as the night,
> Eclipse the lustre of Thy light:
> Keep still in my horizon; for to me
> The sun makes not the day, but Thee.
> . . . Howe'er I rest, great God, let me
> Awake again at last with Thee;
> And thus assured, behold I lie
> Securely, or to wake or die.
> These are my drowsy days; in vain
> I do now wake to sleep again:
> O come that hour when I shall never
> Sleep again, but wake for ever.

SIR THOMAS BROWNE

Human greatness does not lie in wealth or power, but in character and goodness. People are just people, and all people have faults and shortcomings, but all of us are born with a basic goodness.

—ANNE FRANK

Endure hardship with us like a good soldier of Christ Jesus.
2 TIMOTHY 2:3

Where our Captain bids us go,
'Tis not ours to murmur, 'No'.
He that gives the sword and shield,
Chooses too the battle-field
On which we are to fight the foe.
ANONYMOUS

Whatever you do, you need courage. Whatever course you decide upon, there is always someone to tell you that you are wrong. There are always difficulties arising that tempt you to believe your critics are right. To map out a course of action and follow it to an end requires some of the same courage that a soldier needs. Peace has its victories, but it takes brave men and women to win them.

—RALPH WALDO EMERSON

Here on earth we are as soldiers, fighting in a foreign land, that understand not the plan of the campaign, and have no need to understand it; seeing well what is at our hand to be done. Let us do it like soldiers, with submission, with courage, with a heroic joy.

—THOMAS CARLYLE

December 24

Give thanks to the Lord, for he is good; his love endures forever.
PSALMS 118:29

*Let those refuse to sing
Who never knew the Lord;
To Heav'n my thanks will ring
In voiced harmonious chord!*
E. C. M.

Develop an attitude of gratitude, and give thanks for everything that happens to you, knowing that every step forward is a step toward achieving something bigger and better than your current situation.

—BRIAN TRACY

Death and disaster are at our shoulders every second of our lives, trying to get at us. Missing, a lot of the time. A lot of miles on the motorway without a front wheel blow-out. A lot of viruses that slither through our bodies without snagging. A lot of pianos that fall a minute after we've passed. Or a month, it makes no difference. So unless were going to get down on our knees and give thanks every time disaster misses, it makes no sense to moan when it strikes.

—HUGH LAURIE

December 25

*Do not be afraid. I bring you good news of great joy that will be for
all the people. Today in the town of David a Savior
has been born to you; he is Christ the Lord.*
LUKE 1:10-11

How many observe Christ's birthday! How few, His precepts!
BENJAMIN FRANKLIN

My idea of Christmas, whether old-fashioned or modern, is very
simple: loving others. Come to think of it, why do we have to wait
for Christmas to do that?

—BOB HOPE

*I heard the bells on Christmas Day
Their old, familiar carols play,
And wild and sweet
The words repeat
Of peace on earth, good-will to men!*
HENRY WADSWORTH LONGFELLOW

Christmas magic is silent. You don't hear it—you feel it, you know
it, you believe it.

—KEVIN ALAN MILNE

For God was pleased to have all his fullness dwell in him,
and through him to reconcile to himself all things,
whether things on earth or things in heaven,
by making peace through his blood, shed on the cross.
COLOSSIANS 1:19-20

Ah, love, let us be true
To one another! for the world, which seems
To lie before us like a land of dreams,
So various, so beautiful, so new,
Hath really neither joy, nor love, nor light,

Nor certitude, nor peace, nor help for pain;
And we are here as on a darkling plain
Swept with confused alarms of struggle and flight,
Where ignorant armies clash by night.
MATTHEW ARNOLD

This is the greatest gift God can give you: to understand what
happened in your life. To have it explained. It is the peace you have
been searching for.

—MITCH ALBOM

December 27

*As a father has compassion on his children,
so the Lord has compassion on those who fear him . . .*
PSALMS 103:13

You cannot save people. You can only love them.
ANAIS NIN

Every single person has at least one secret that would break your heart. If we could just remember this, I think there would be a lot more compassion and tolerance in the world.

—FRANK WARREN

Waking up this morning, I smile. Twenty-four brand new hours are before me. I vow to live fully in each moment and to look at all beings with eyes of compassion.

—THICH NHAT HANHA

December 28

So, firm in steadfast hope, in thought secure,
in full accord to all Thy world of joy,
May I be nerved to labors high and pure,
And thou Thy child to do Thy work employ.

J. STERLING

The return from your work must be the satisfaction which that work brings you and the world's need of that work. With this life is heaven, or as near heaven as you can get.

—W. E. B. DUBOIS

We know only too well that what we are doing is nothing more than a drop in the ocean. But if the drop were not there, the ocean would be missing something.

—MOTHER TERESA

Nothing will work unless you do.

—MAYA ANGELOU

December 29

Finally brothers, whatever is true, whatever is noble, whatever is right, whatever is pure, whatever is lovely, whatever is admirable—if anything is excellent or praiseworthy—think about such things.

PHILIPPIANS 4:8

Love thyself last: cherish those hearts that hate thee;
Corruption wins not more than honesty.
Still in thy right hand carry gentle peace,
To silence envious tongues: be just, and fear not.
Let all the ends thou aim'st at be thy country's,
Thy God's, and truth's . . .
WILLIAM SHAKESPEARE

When we are young we are often puzzled by the fact that each person we admire seems to have a different version of what life ought to be, what a good man is, how to live, and so on. If we are especially sensitive it seems more than puzzling, it is disheartening. What most people usually do is to follow one person's ideas and then another's depending on who looms largest on one's horizon at the time. The one with the deepest voice, the strongest appearance, the most authority and success, is usually the one who gets our momentary allegiance; and we try to pattern our ideals after him. But as life goes on we get a perspective on this and all these different versions of truth become a little pathetic. Each person thinks that he has the formula for triumphing over life's limitations and knows with authority what it means to be a man, and he usually tries to win a following for his particular patent. Today we know that people try so hard to win converts for their point of view because it is more than merely an outlook on life: it is an immortality formula.

—ERNEST BECKER

Any faith that admires truth, that strives to know God, must be brave enough to accommodate the universe.

—CARL SAGAN

December 30

As you have heard from the beginning,
his command is that you walk in love.
2 JOHN 1:6

Mirth is like a flash of lightning, that breaks through a gloom of clouds, and glitters for a moment; cheerfulness keeps up a kind of daylight in the mind, and fills it with a steady and perpetual serenity.

—JOSEPH ADDISON

God is life. God is life in action. The best way to say, "I love you, God," is to live your life doing your best. The best way to say, "Thank you, God," is by letting go of the past and living in the present moment, right here and now. Whatever life takes away from you, let it go. When you surrender and let go of the past, you allow yourself to be fully alive in the moment. Letting go of the past means you can enjoy the dream that is happening right now.

—MIGUEL RUIZ

December 31

Forgetting what is behind and straining toward what is ahead,
I press on toward the goal . . .
PHILIPPIANS 3:14

The time of life is short;
To spend that shortness basely were too long.
WILLIAM SHAKESPEARE

That ye may live, which will be many days,
Both in one faith unanimous; though sad
With cause for evils past, yet much more cheered
With meditation on the happy end.

JOHN MILTON

It is not by regretting what is irreparable that true work is to be done, but by making the best, of what we are. It is not by complaining that we have not the right tools, but by using well the tools we have. What we are, and where we are, is God's providential arrangement, God's doing, though it may be man's misdoing; and the manly and the wise way is to look your disadvantages in the face, and see what can be made out of them. Life, like war, is a series of mistakes, and he is not the best Christian nor the best general who makes the fewest false steps. He is the best who wins the most splendid victories by the retrieval of mistakes. Forget mistakes; organize victory out of mistakes.

—F. W. ROBERTSON